# OUT
## *of the*
# SILENCE

# DUANE
# MILLER

A
JANET
THOMA
BOOK

THOMAS NELSON PUBLISHERS
Nashville • Atlanta • London • Vancouver
Printed in the United States of America

Published in Nashville, Tennessee, by Thomas Nelson, Inc.

The Bible version used in this publication is THE NEW KING JAMES VERSION. Copyright © 1979, 1980, 1982, 1990 Thomas Nelson, Inc., Publishers.

### Library of Congress Cataloging-in-Publication Data

Miller, Duane.
   Out of the silence : a personal testimony of God's healing Power / Duane Miller ; with Gary Thomas.
      p. cm.
   Includes bibliographical references.
   ISBN 0-7852-7407-3
   1. Miller, Duane. 2. Baptists—United States—Clergy—Biography. 3. Spiritual healing—Case studies. Mutism—Case studies. I. Thomas, Gary. II. Title.
BX6495.M45A3 1997
234'.131'092—dc21
[B]
                                                    96-36852
                                                       CIP

Printed in the United States of America.
5 6 — 01 00 99 98

# Dedication

To Joylene:

My faithful wife, my fellow-laborer in ministry, my favorite prayer partner, my affectionate companion, and my very best friend.

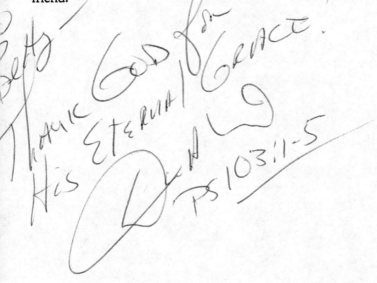

# Contents

# Acknowledgments

There are many people who have knowingly or unknowingly had a part in making this book possible. For those whose names are omitted by oversight, please indulge me with your forgiveness.

First of all, thanks to Gary Thomas for hard work on a short schedule. You performed marvelously.

The medical staff at Baylor College of Medicine in Houston, Texas, was my lead team throughout this ordeal. Their care and concern, not only for my physical problems, but my psyche as well, was more blessed than they will ever know.

Thanks to Jodie Berndt for introductions and to Janet Thoma for believing in the project. Many thanks to Kathi Mills who assisted greatly in the organization and drafting of this book.

I owe greatly the leadership and members of the Catacombs Class at Houston's First Baptist Church without whom there would have been no forum for the story to have taken place. Also, to the Christian Education leadership of the church for "taking a chance" on me.

Thanks to the congregation of First Baptist Church in Brenham, Texas, for their prayers and support during the beginning of the journey and for the continued prayers and contacts after my wife and I resigned. You blessed our lives, and we love you.

I am grateful to Rev. Ivar Frick, my childhood pastor, who laid the foundation of faith in my life. I learned more from him than either of us suspected.

Many, many thanks to Dr. John Bisagno, senior pastor at Houston's First Baptist Church. Your care concern, prayers, confidence, faith, and support for this ministry have meant more than I can express. I love my pastor!

Thanks to Mom and Dad Correll for never losing hope. Thanks, Mother, for never doubting. Thanks to all three of you for dogged, determined faith in Almighty God.

Thanks, Lisa and Jodi, for forgiving me.

Finally, thanks to my Lord Jesus Christ for allowing me to work in His church.

# Preface

The story you are about to read is so incredible that, had it not happened to me, I would be tempted not to believe it. But it *did* happen to me, and was witnessed by some two hundred people. It was also reviewed, studied, and written about by some of the most distinguished medical practitioners in the world.

Though this miracle changed my life in many wonderful ways, even more important, I believe, is the fact that it has changed the lives of countless others—and it can change your life as well. There was nothing special about my circumstances, faith, or abilities that would lead God to touch me more than He might touch others, including you. The exciting truth is, the only explanation for what happened was the good favor of a sovereign God who loves His children.

And God loves you every bit as much as He loves me.

As you experience the depths of my anguish and the explosion of joy at my deliverance, keep in mind that God never does anything without having a purpose. There's a message in my story *for you*.

# chapter one

# The
# *Sounds of*
# *Silence*

I NEVER SUSPECTED THAT MY LIFE WOULD need such a fantastic miracle; certainly, the thought of what I was about to endure never crossed my mind as I awoke on a Sunday morning, January 14, 1990. Except for the onset of the flu, the day seemed like any other. There was no particular sign from heaven, no intuitive warning, nothing to tip me off that my life was about to enter a dark season of silence.

The twenty-hour days I had been working had finally caught up with me. My body hurt all over. My throat was scratchy, my head was stuffy, and I was in that netherworld of not quite having the flu yet, but knowing that it was coming. All I really wanted to do was stay in bed.

There was just one problem with that scenario. I was senior pastor of the First Baptist Church in Brenham, Texas, and was scheduled to preach both morning services. Bed was a luxury that would have to wait. Because I was feeling so poorly, however, I allowed myself to hang onto the covers a little longer than usual, arriving at the church at about 7 A.M. I drank some tea with the hope that it might lubricate my throat enough to get me through the day's requirements. The dizzy sensation you get when sickness first begins to take hold of your body began to spread through me as I sat at my desk, but I kept thinking and praying, *Please, Lord, not now; I've got two sermons to preach.*

My motivation to go on was based on much more than just the day's schedule, however. Over the past four years, God had given me a deep love for this church, and I wanted to see it succeed. Teaching God's Word wasn't just a vocation for me; it was my passion, and it's fair to say that I felt more alive in the pulpit than just about anywhere else. It might sound corny, but if you could see my heart you would know that my sermons were love letters more than they were lectures—bouquets God had given me with which to bless this wonderful group of people who made up the First Baptist Church.

But just like any church, we weren't without our problems. Before I arrived, the congregation had embarked on a building campaign that had now gone awry. As the new senior pastor, I had inherited over one million dollars' worth of debt. That fact alone would be enough to frighten away many a prospective pastor, but with my background in business, I felt equipped (and determined) to get us back on solid financial footing.

We were making progress, but it was taking its toll on me. Getting a handle on our finances, preaching four times a week, participating in what seemed like endless committee meetings, and performing what pastoral visitations I could fit in (and feeling guilty for those I wanted to do but didn't have time for) had resulted in my putting in twenty-hour days. I certainly don't recommend this, but at the time, I reasoned that it was the temporary price that had to be paid to get the church onto more solid footing, financially and spiritually.

My sermon for the morning was entitled, "Jesus, Just the Mention of Your Name." I planned to end the sermon with the song by the same name. This was not an unusual thing for me to do, since I had begun singing professionally when I was sixteen years old, and I loved nothing better. Singing was the way I worshiped and the way I expressed what I felt inside. I loved my congregation, and I loved my Lord; singing was my way of loving them both at the same time.

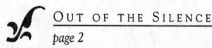

The tea had temporarily loosened my throat enough to begin the service. As I began preaching, however, my voice started "catching" on words. I kept trying to discreetly clear my throat, but let me tell you—it's a supernatural gift of God to quietly clear your throat when you're wearing a lapel microphone and preaching to a Sunday morning crowd. That morning, I didn't have that gift!

Finally, the sermon was over and I went into the song. It took no more than a few bars for me to realize my range was drastically limited. When I hit the last note, I flatted it terribly. Even a professional singer can occasionally let loose a zinger; I wasn't shocked about that. But, for the first time in my life, I couldn't correct it. My voice simply wouldn't respond.

That concerned me a bit, but I didn't dwell on it. I wrote it off to a sore throat and nothing more. I would have never believed that I wouldn't sing another song for over three years.

After the first service, my throat grew more painful by the minute. Between services, I hastily went through my notes, deleting every word and paragraph in my sermon that wasn't absolutely essential. It had now become painful to speak each word, so every syllable had to count. Singing a song at the end was completely out of the question. I'd be delighted just to get through an abbreviated message.

During the second sermon, my throat only grudgingly let go of each word, making every sound and inflection grate on the back of my throat like sandpaper. I gave the shortest sermon of my life.

Afterwards, I felt somewhat apologetic, as if I had cheated my congregation for speaking so briefly. A deacon, however, gave me a slightly different perspective when he said, "Well hallelujah, Pastor, this is the first Sunday we've gotten out of church on time in four years!"

I smiled, patted him on the back, and wondered how I'd get through a crucial committee meeting that afternoon. The dizziness of the flu had begun to spread, so I really had to concentrate as people came up to shake my hand.

*Duane Miller*

I drove home, and my wife, Joylene, fixed some honey-lemon tea. Eating was out of the question.

An hour or so later, I was back at the church for the committee meeting. As men and women spoke enthusiastically about various aspects of our missions program, I fought the effects of alternating hot flashes and cold spells. I was still dizzy, and it took everything I had to concentrate on what was being said. The meeting seemed to go on forever, and the final "amen" of the closing prayer was uttered just before the evening service was scheduled to start. I realized I couldn't stand, much less preach for thirty minutes, so as Charlie, one of our deacons, walked by, I gently grabbed his arm and pulled him aside. "Charlie," I said, "I'm just too sick to preach this service. I can't handle it."

Charlie knew my work habits, and he knew that I wouldn't do this if there were any way around it. He also knew the service was scheduled to start in about five minutes. Still, he smiled, said, "Don't worry, Preach, I'll handle it. You just relax," and clapped me on the back.

I love teasing deacons. It's one of the very best perks of being a senior pastor. And the mark of a good deacon is his ability to throw it right back. But that night, all the fun dissolved into admiration, thankfulness, and joy as I watched Charlie Matejowsky deliver a world-class sermon on less than ten minutes' notice.

After the evening service, the church prayed for me and sent me home. Ultimately, their prayers would be answered. None of us imagined that it would take *so long*, however. And my heart would have been broken if I had known that I had preached my last sermon and conducted my last committee meeting as this church's senior pastor.

## WHITE CHOCOLATE REPRIEVE

The flu hung on for five straight days. I felt like a mummy in a bad B-movie horror flick. A member of our congregation—a dear friend and wonderful physician—gave me some medi-

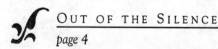

cine to treat the symptoms and added, "Duane, your body has said, 'Shut down and rest.' Don't even think about preaching on Sunday."

I couldn't have if I'd wanted to. Not only could I not swallow without pain, I couldn't even *breathe* without pain, and I had never experienced that before. I tried everything to bring relief: cough drops, hot tea, peppermint oil, baking soda concoctions, you name it. Any Baptist church is full of homegrown remedies for sore throats, and I tried them all!

Eating was impossible, and Joylene started to get worried. "You have to eat *something*," she insisted.

I thought about it, and then a smile spread across my face. Joylene read it perfectly. "All right," she said, smiling back. "White chocolate almond it is."

Brenham, Texas, is the home of Blue Bell ice cream. If you haven't tasted Blue Bell ice cream, you haven't tasted ice cream at its best. Blue Bell is so good that Ben and Jerry's, Baskin-Robbins, and Häagen-Dazs taste like paste in comparison. Once you've had Blue Bell, you're ruined. And white chocolate almond—well, all I can say is, if I was going to endure the agony of a swallow, only the taste of Blue Bell white chocolate almond ice cream would make the struggle worth it. (The Lord and I have discussed the matter thoroughly, and He has assured me that Blue Bell ice cream will be featured at the Great Supper.)

The only problem was, Joylene couldn't find my favorite flavor anywhere. She went to every grocery and specialty store in the Brenham area looking for white chocolate almond. Everybody was out.

Finally, she called my secretary and asked her if she knew any place or anyone that had any. Cecil (that really is her name) didn't, but in just a little while she showed up at our door with a half-gallon of Homemade Vanilla, a sack of almonds, and a couple bars of white chocolate.

"Here," she said. "At least you can make your own." Always resourceful, ever helpful; that's Cecil Otto.

 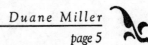

Within a few more days, however, my throat became so sore that even white chocolate almond wasn't enough to tempt me to eat. I had to force liquids down, but each time I swallowed, the water or tea felt like daggers maliciously attacking my throat. I wanted to cry every time I took a sip.

Not only was I in agony physically—having to choose between a desert-dry throat and what felt like a stint as a clumsy circus sword swallower—but I began to suffer withdrawal from work. Remember, I had grown used to twenty-hour days. I slept for four days straight at the beginning of my illness, but even after that my mind wasn't clear enough to work. I couldn't read, so I'd sit and stare and occasionally watch some sports on television. ESPN and the news were about the only breaks I was afforded in a generally miserable existence.

After ten days, the rest of my flu symptoms abated, but my throat was still on fire and my voice was reduced to a slight, raspy whisper. I would have taken all the flu symptoms back if in so doing I could have regained a healthy throat. I was so tired of bracing for the pain every time I took a drink. To make matters worse, the pain evolved to include constriction. To get some idea of what it felt like, put this book down and wrap both hands around your throat with your thumbs nestled under your chin. Squeeze in with your thumbs and lift up with your fingers. Notice how you suddenly have to swallow? Now imagine that the swallow feels like a donkey kicking you in the wind pipe. Imagine that this went on, and on, and on, sometimes making you wonder if you had enough of a throat left to take a breath.

That's how I felt for ten days.

I finally called my longtime friend and singer Roger McDuff, and he recommended a specialist that he had seen. As a pastor, I know some sectors of the church think that consulting the medical profession is a compromise of faith, or at least evidence of a lack of faith. I have never believed that. While I obviously believe that God heals, I also believe He has given us the medical profession as helpful agents. I suppose I could pray that God would fix my car's carburetor, but don't you think God wants me to visit a mechanic, just to make sure? Is it really any different with our bodies?

I don't think it is, even though some sectors of the church have a hard time accepting this—at least in theory. A number of years ago, one of the prominent faith teachers who had chastised Christians for consulting physicians began to succumb to a serious malady. He was forced to leave the country in order to seek medical help surreptitiously. When your doctrine forces you to become a hypocrite in order to appear consistent, it may be time to change your doctrine!

My story is not one of overcoming faith. I did nothing, I believed nothing, I achieved nothing, to warrant God's incredible touch. Instead, my story is of the dynamic power and grace of a merciful, loving, and sovereign God.

## PERMANENT FEARS

I was inwardly begging God for relief as I made my way into the doctor's office. I met a professional-looking man in his early fifties. His slight height, about 5-foot-8, made me feel welcome (Shaquille O'Neal could use me as an armrest). He had dark hair, heavy eyebrows, and the bearing of a Middle Easterner.

The doctor tried to examine my throat with a scope, but it was so swollen that he couldn't get the scope down.

"This doesn't look good," he said.

*It doesn't look good?* I thought. *You ought to try feeling it.*

"Duane," he added, "I don't know how you can even breathe, there's so much infection in your throat. It's very swollen."

He clicked his tongue, and after filling one hip with a shot of antibiotics and the other hip with a steroid shot, he wrote out a prescription for a continuing series of each. The doctor suspected, even then, that the virus may have penetrated the myelin sheath that insulates the nerves in the vocal cords. To get a picture of this, imagine a copper wire. That's a nerve. Now imagine black, rubber insulation around the wire. That's the myelin sheath. If you gently squeeze the two with a pair of pliers, you may indent the insulation, but the wire inside it remains unharmed. That's what usually happens when a virus invades your body. It may "indent" the insulation around the nerves, but it rarely invades the nerve itself.

Just as the indent in the rubber wire eventually works its way back out, so the myelin sheath eventually returns to normal. In my case, the doctor feared, the virus had managed to penetrate the insulation of the myelin sheath and affect the nerves controlling the vocal cords.

The doctor didn't tell me that then, for good reason. He didn't want to scare me until he was absolutely sure of the diagnosis. If he was right, he knew the damage would be permanent. Rather than alarm me, he wanted to see how I'd respond to the medication.

Thus began my life without a voice.

## THE INVISIBLE MAN

I never realized how central a voice is to everyday life in the modern world. When it's there, you don't realize how much you use it. When it's gone, you become amazed at how limited you are. It's sort of like when you injure a finger and then become amazed at how you took a pain-free finger for granted. Suddenly, every time you pick something up, the nerves in the finger scream at you, though you never even thought about using that finger before.

We take our voice for granted as well. Imagine, for instance, having your banking hours cut to before 2 P.M. I could no longer use the drive-through. If Joylene and I wanted to stop for a hamburger, she had to lean over and yell into Ronald McDonald's face to place the order. If I needed Joylene and she was upstairs, I had to walk up and get her; I couldn't call to her. If my kids were doing something foolish, I couldn't yell out; I had to walk over and use hand signals to get their attention. Conversation on the phone became virtually impossible; whispers don't translate very well over phone lines.

Even when I did something as simple as buy gasoline, I had to be careful that I didn't stop at a station where the attendant was in a glass booth. My voice didn't carry through the small screens they have set up. Joylene did her best to protect my dignity, but it's frankly embarrassing when your wife has to do all your talking for you, or your wife gets out to pay the gas, as if you're just too lazy to walk over and do it.

It's one thing to live like this for a few days, but as the days turned into weeks it got really frustrating. One time I was the only one home when the phone rang. I had nothing to do and would have loved to have talked to somebody, but I knew I had to let the answering machine pick it up. If I answered the phone, the person on the other end would hear only silence and assume they had a bad connection.

I had gotten used to this, except that this time, my mother's voice cut into the silence. I felt like somebody had punched me in the stomach. I'm my mother's only child, and she needed me. I was also feeling lonely and would have loved the diversion of an afternoon chat. I almost wanted to scream as I heard her voice, but this only frustrated me all the more, as screaming was the *last* thing I could do.

I felt like the invisible man. People had sat in churches, hundreds or thousands at a time, to hear me speak or sing. I had been on radio, and tens of thousands of people had heard my voice in their cars and homes.

Now, I couldn't even get through to my mom. I wanted to smash the phone with a hammer right there. Instead, I sat by the phone, holding back the tears, and started wondering when this madness would end.

But, really, the madness was just beginning.

# Is This
# Really
# Happening?

MY YOUNGEST DAUGHTER,
JODI, IS A schoolteacher. Just
before she began her teaching
career, Baylor University asked an experienced
teacher to speak to the graduating seniors about
what life would be like in a "real" classroom.

This woman's initial assignment was a first
grade class. She went to work that first morning,
somewhat nervous, but all went well—until lunchtime. When
she excused the class to go to lunch, everyone filed out except
for one little boy, who instead began to pack up his crayons,
pencils, and papers.

"Where are you going?" the new teacher asked him.

"Home," he announced with a finality that surprised her.

"But why?"

"I always go home when the other kids go to lunch."

His teacher smiled at him. "That was last year, honey, when
you were in kindergarten. You're in first grade now, and you get
to stay here *all day*. You eat lunch here with the other kids, then
come back to class and we'll study all afternoon."

The little boy looked up at her, frowned, put his hands on
his hips, clenched his teeth, and demanded, "Well, who signed
me up for that?"

We chuckle at the little boy's naïveté. The agenda he had set for his day was completely rearranged by forces beyond his control, and entirely without his consultation or permission, and he was incensed.

But, if the truth be known, haven't we all asked that question at some point in our lives? When a situation presents itself and our lives are suddenly redirected, aren't we like that young man in our questioning of the source and wisdom of our circumstances? Don't we demand to know, "Who signed me up for that?"

I sure did. I'm not one who runs for the doctors; if anything, I have a tendency to wait too long. But when you're as sick as I was, and it keeps hanging on, you just want to get better.

After two weeks of dutifully taking the medication, I returned to the doctor, a little less patient than I was fourteen days earlier. Some improvement had been made. The infection was gone and the swelling was gone, but the constrictive pressure remained. I still lived with a choking sensation and I still couldn't speak clearly.

Because the swelling had gone down, the doctor was able to get a "hard scope" down my throat to take a look around. He had me admitted to the hospital, then put to sleep. Having the patient sedated allows the doctor to put a hard scope deep into the patient's throat without initiating a gag reflex. The hard scope earns its name by being hard, and it's about as gentle as a brick. I still felt its imprint a week after the doctor had pulled it out. I went to the doctors to get well, but instead, I ended up feeling worse!

I mention this to help people who have never faced serious medical care to understand the travail of their ill loved ones. On top of being sick, patients often have to recover from the medical treatment itself. It's one of the great ironies of modern medicine, but the indignities and soreness that arise from extensive care can cause people to become even more weary.

My doctor realized that my condition was beyond his expertise, so he referred me to the Baylor College of Medicine in

Houston, Texas. This was difficult to hear. For weeks, I had been persevering by promising myself that the ordeal would soon be over. My mind can work like a steel trap: I simply forbade myself the luxury of thinking about "what if" scenarios. Up to this point, I hadn't even broached the question of *whether* I was going to be healed; it was always a matter of *when*.

It's tough to remain in denial when a doctor admits he's in over his head. I could no longer pretend that this was just a little virus that would eventually dissolve into my body.

On the other hand, I was hopeful about going to Houston. Many people don't realize that Houston is virtually the medical capital of the world. The Baylor College of Medicine, the University of Texas Medical School, and the Prairie View A&M School of Nursing are all located in the same area. If something can't be done or cured in Houston, it probably can't be done or cured at all.

The huge buildings surrounding the Methodist hospital made me feel even smaller than I am. As I pulled open the door to walk inside, however, I was anxious for the "specialists" to "fix me up" and send me back to my church in Brenham. I had been out of the pulpit for over a month and was ready to get back to work.

When I was accepted at Baylor, I found that I had "inherited" a team of some thirteen doctors and staff. Terms like *otolaryngologist, neurologist, speech pathologist,* and *speech therapist* had never been a part of my language, but in the days ahead these were the people whose expertise could give me back my world.

Or so I thought.

The hard scope test had proven to be nothing more than the hors d'oeuvres. My body endured test after test after test. I was poked, prodded, examined, photographed, and charted until I felt like a frog in a junior high lab. The doctors performed CAT scans. I experienced my first MRI, in which you're put into a tube, the top of which is no more than three inches from your face, and you endure a loud banging noise for up to an hour (a claustrophobic's worst nightmare). I had to take special medication. On one occasion I had electrodes taped to my body and was monitored for 4 1/2 months. I went through urinalysis tests, filling a bottle morning, noon, and night. Everything I ate was monitored. I gave more blood than I thought I had in me, sometimes twice a week.

I took hearing tests. I had to stand on one foot with my eyes closed to test my balance. I was hooked up for an EEG and had to go to sleep while wired to a machine—no small feat, I assure you. They sent dye through my body and monitored it as it passed through me.

In short, every aspect of my life was invaded, reviewed, and discussed. Physically, I lived what the last judgment must feel like spiritually. It was a bit scary for a medical layman like me.

Finally, after one of the doctors recommended yet another test, I asked him, "What are you looking for here?"

"A tumor," the doctor replied.

*A tumor!* I thought. *That means cancer.*

Is there anything our culture fears more than the "C" word? Anyone who has been involved in pastoring for any length of time has seen the ravages of that ugly disease. I've seen grown men reduced to the status of children as their families look on the emaciated body of their loved one with disbelief. I've seen some of the richest voices stolen, the strongest bodies wilted, and the most glorious hair disappear in the wake of that insatiable disease.

Samuel Johnson wrote that "disease generally begins that equality which death completes." Was I to join the legions who have been robbed by cancer? I started out assuming I had the flu, and then maybe strep throat. Never did I consider something like . . . *cancer.*

I began praying, *Lord, what are you doing? You gave me the call to preach. You gave me the strength, the time, and the opportunity. I should be at the peak of my ministry, but now I can't even order a hamburger!*

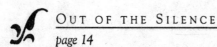

Don't get me wrong. I believe in the sovereignty of God. I just wanted to understand what was happening, so I found myself asking, Why me? Why this? Why now?

I wasn't praying to be let out of the box, only that God would help me to understand what He was doing. You see, I'm a control freak. I *need* to understand what's going on. I'm willing to endure punishment, but even then, I want some measure of command. When I was little, my daddy would always give me two choices: a whipping with a belt or one week of being grounded. I *always* chose the belt. *Let's get this over with*, I'd think. *Then we can move on.*

That's how I felt now, with God. *Let's just get this over with, please?*

As difficult as it was for me, it was even more difficult for Joylene. When she heard the word *cancer*, she just gulped.

"When will we know?" she asked.

"A couple days," I said.

"I'm going with you." Joylene's tone was such that I knew not to argue.

## THE EXILE

When the results were ready, Joylene accompanied me to the doctor's office to get the news firsthand. Time moved slowly as we settled into the chairs in my lead physician's office. We desperately wanted to hear what he had to say, but at the same time, the possibilities scared us. Fortunately, the doctor began immediately getting down to business.

"Duane," he said, "I don't know what the problem is, but I am certain what it is not. You do not have cancer."

Joylene wept. I reached over and took her hand. God was knitting my heart to this fantastic woman in new and wonderful ways. We were facing awful challenges, but Joylene was right there beside me. Fortunately, the uncertainty and pain was making both of us fall passionately in love with each other once again rather than pushing us apart.

*Duane Miller*

Joylene and I went home, weeping and thanking God that I didn't have cancer. I remember thinking, *Nothing could be as bad as having cancer. Whatever it is, since it isn't cancer, these wonderful doctors will diagnose me, treat me, and have me on my way in short order.*

*Thank you Lord,* I kept praying, *it's not that.* I didn't even want to say the word.

The tests kept coming, and the doctors kept scratching their heads. We went through several months of regular examinations, and the doctors' next suspicion was stress.

As they reviewed my history—invariably raising their eyebrows when they got to the twenty-hour-days part—they said that sometimes stress can result in the vocal symptom I was experiencing.

"Duane," the doctor said, "it may be that your body is just plain worn out. You've been working so many hours and you're under such stress that it may be affecting your ability to talk. We want you to take some time off."

I hadn't taken a vacation in almost three years—and that was when my father-in-law had cancer. "I don't know," I said. "I've already been off for several months. I'm not sure a vacation will help."

"Duane," the doctor was speaking firmly now, "we're not talking about a vacation. We're talking about a six-month leave of absence."

*Six-month leave of absence!* He was right. He wasn't talking about a vacation. He was talking about an exile!

Given the financial situation of our congregation, I couldn't imagine how they could afford to give me a six-month leave of absence. Furthermore, there are always unresolved issues in every congregation, and our church was no exception. Certain matters could be put on the shelf for a few weeks, but six months? What about my plans? What about my dreams?

"Look, Duane, I understand that this sounds like a long time," the doctor continued. "I'd be willing to talk to your church for you and explain the need for you to be absolutely silent."

*Six months of absolute silence?* Did I just hear him correctly? This well-meaning attempt to "comfort" me had the opposite effect. I came here to get better, and now I'm being told that I'm not supposed to speak for six months!

I was shell-shocked. When the doctor kept looking at me, I realized he had just asked me a question. It was a very generous offer to speak to my church, but I thought explaining my situation to the church was something I should do.

"Thank you, doctor," I croaked out. "That's not necessary. I'll tell them."

It had been five months since I had last preached at Brenham. Now, it would be at least another six. How could I face my congregation?

The next Sunday, I walked up to my pulpit and looked out at the dear faces sitting before me. I saw several elderly members and wondered if I'd ever see some of them again. (As it turned out, two did die before I returned.) I saw a new family that had just started coming—they were a great couple with two fantastic children, exactly the kind of folks you want to build a church around—and I began wondering if they'd still be there when I returned.

I made my announcement as best I could with my raspy, quiet voice. Six months ago, I could thunder from this pulpit for two hours and three services every Sunday and still leave eager for more. This morning, after less than ten minutes, I was exhausted.

There was a mixed reaction. Some of the people wondered what could be accomplished by taking another six months off after I'd already been out for five. I could understand their concerns completely; I had the same ones! Others were concerned about the leadership vacuum. Though I hadn't been able to preach, my expected return was enough to keep things in order, but nobody could imagine what another six months would bring.

Even so, after the service, members came up and embraced Joylene and me and poured out their well wishes. "Hey, Preacher, we're on your side. Go get well." I thanked them. Their faces had such a precious sincerity that it made leaving all the more difficult.

Finally, the well-wishers' line was past. Only a few cars remained in the parking lot. I saw one of the men in our church whose walk with God and administrative skills I particularly admired. I whistled and motioned with my hand. He turned and walked over to me.

"David," I said, "take care of the church. Don't let feelings get out of hand. Protect these folks for me."

"Just get well," he said as he grasped my shoulders. "We'll be all right."

We walked to our car, and I managed to slip into the front seat before the first tear made its way down my cheek. The only thing worse than saying good-bye to your church is saying good-bye to a family member. Joylene reached over and put a hand on my shoulder. I turned the keys in the ignition and backed up, all the while wondering, *Is this really happening?*

# Three
# Vacations
# and a Funeral

S IX MONTHS OFF TO DO WHAT-EVER I felt like doing. That sounds terrific, except that what I wanted to do most—preach, sing, and pastor—I couldn't do. I didn't want to go to Disneyland. After the previous five months, I just wanted to work as a pastor!

"Okay, Duane," the doctors were very insistent just before I left. "You're to be as quiet as possible for the entire six months. There should be absolutely no unnecessary talking."

Of my one hundred favorite things to do, being silent isn't one of them. In fact, of the first thousand things I'd think of, a silent retreat wouldn't find its way on the list—certainly not a silent retreat for six months.

Facing the inevitable, however, Joylene went to the toy store and bought some Magic Slates—toy boards that you write on, and then lift up to erase. We developed our own system of shorthand and learned to communicate reasonably well. Whenever we went into a restaurant, I'd write down my order and Joylene would speak it. If she asked me what I wanted to do, I'd pick up the Magic Slate, fight the urge to write "TALK!" and make a suggestion.

As our exile began, some good friends from Houston offered us their vacation home in Galveston, Texas, where we had stayed many times before. In fact, this vacation home had sheltered some of the happiest moments of our lives as a family, so it seemed like the natural place to go.

The Gulf Coast was beautiful, the home was comfortable as always, and everything was in place for us to enjoy a fantastic vacation. Instead, however, I paced the floor like a caged animal.

Joylene went into hyperdrive to keep me occupied. She was phenomenal. She acted like a camp counselor, knowing that I'd want to call the church if we ever slowed down. "Let's rent bicycles!" she'd suggest, and I'd go along. We went surf fishing, we visited the train museum, we went to an 1800s shopping area—all the touristy things that vacationers do in Galveston. My daughters, Jodi and Lisa, came down for the weekend, and we took them out to dinner and then walked on the beach.

That night I got a call from my church at Brenham. Before we left Brenham, we had set up a system whereby at least three deacons would know where I was at all times. I insisted to Joylene and the doctors that I simply couldn't divorce the church; I had to know what was going on. They gave their approval, as long as I didn't get involved.

During these "checkup" calls, Joylene did the talking. I listened in on a second phone, heard the questions, then wrote down my answers on a Magic Slate.

On this particular evening, the deacon spoke softly, so I knew something was wrong. "Duane," he began. Almost intuitively, I could guess what was coming. "Bessie Jean has passed away."

I felt like a bus had hit me. Dear, sweet Bessie Jean, the wife of one of my closest friends in the church, had died.

As a pastor, I would have known exactly what to do. I'd have thrown on some presentable clothes, gathered my car keys, and been at her husband's door within minutes. I never really had to learn how to cope with grief without working, because my role as a pastor mandated that I kick into high gear whenever such a situation presented itself. Certainly I grieved, and grieved deeply, but this time it was different.

For the first time in my life, I had to be still while I mourned. I had to stay quiet, not move, and work through all the confusing and painful emotions without the luxury of activity to keep my mind preoccupied.

It was agonizing to realize I couldn't even go back to do her funeral. The doctors absolutely forbade it; and even if I did go back, I couldn't speak, so what good would I be?

Guilt poured over me like the crashing waves that pummeled the sand outside our front door. *I'm supposed to be having fun,* I thought, *but I'm more miserable than I've ever been.*

Early the next morning I woke up and walked onto the beach. The sun was just coming up. We had been in Galveston for about a week, and I had come to a depressing conclusion. Fun just wasn't fun anymore. Over the past few days, I had felt like an incredibly hungry man who was being offered ultrasweet cake. Any other time, I would have eaten the cake with abandon. But when you're really hungry, you want something with substance.

While I was in a "fun" location and doing "fun" things, the substance that gives "fun" its meaning was completely gone. I could see my daughters, but I couldn't talk to them. I could take my wife to a restaurant, but I couldn't order for her. I could see beautiful sights, but I couldn't verbally share them with anyone else. By the time I got my Magic Slate out, the animal or landmark had passed.

As I walked around the beach house, I thought of the potluck dinners, the late-night jigsaw puzzles, the giddiness of playing with the kids on the beach. We had enjoyed tremendous times here, but the power of their memory now mocked me. The unquestioned happiness of those sunny days in Galveston taunted me every time I closed my eyes.

I wanted to scream.

Have you ever felt that way? So frustrated that you just want to shout? Now imagine if that's the *last* thing you can do. Even my frustration got me worked up.

It was the first time I really felt undone. By no means would it be the last, but it was certainly the first. The tears gathered pressure behind my eyes. I closed my lids until the pressure was too great. When I was forced to open them again, it was like a huge faucet had just been released. Memories of Bessie Jean, memories of happy times, memories of singing songs . . .

I wept until my shoulders started shaking. I don't know how long I stood there, but after a while, I felt Joylene's arms around me, just holding me, and I needed to be held.

"This isn't working, is it?" she said. Her voice was soft, just as I needed it to be.

I shook my head. "You got that right."

"Let's go to Missouri."

My wife knew what she was doing. Galveston was less than two hours from Brenham. Being so close but not being able to attend to the church's needs was killing me. Missouri was over twelve hours away. There was nothing I could do there. Its distance was its sanity, at least for my situation.

I nodded my head, and Joylene turned to go pack our bags.

## FAMILIAR HAUNTS

When I think of Missouri, I think of fishing. Joylene's parents live tucked away in the southwest corner of the state, among some of the finest lakes in the country. Joylene's dad and I always get along extremely well, and I was actually looking forward to spending time out on the lake where silence is more the rule than the exception.

I had gone to school in Missouri, so we had a lot of friends there, and Joylene reasoned quite naturally that being among good friends would take my mind off present travails. Word about my situation had spread quickly. Loved ones from the past came by as soon as they heard we were in town.

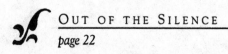

What shocked both them and me, however, was the growing recognition that I was not the man I used to be. Joylene and I have always been known as a "fun" couple. I love to play practical jokes, and wisecracks just come natural to me. Surrounded by our longtime friends, a wisecrack would come to mind and I'd try to croak it out, laughing to myself as I forced the words out.

"What?" everyone would stop and ask.

I repeated myself as best I could.

"I'm sorry, I didn't get the last part," someone would say.

I threw up my hands. The humor was long since gone. (Wisecracks age in about five seconds, and it was taking me at least a minute to make myself understood.)

My interest in having fun bottomed out. It was too much work! Trying to stay upbeat, swallowing funny replies, not being able to join in the conversation without seriously disrupting it—it just wasn't worth the effort. Instead, I sat back and became an observer.

That was the evenings. The mornings were just as bad. I'd wake up after a full night's sleep, spend some time with the Lord and Scripture, and a great thought or sermon idea would come to mind. Well, what was the problem with that? you might ask.

Remember, I had gone months without preaching a sermon. From preaching four times a week, I went to preaching zero times a week. Though my gift of teaching hadn't been stopped, my physical ability to do so had. Consequently, I felt about ten years pregnant, spiritually speaking. Sermon ideas, outlines, illustrations, and passages came into my mind and then sat there until they spoiled. Instead of fresh bread with which to feed a flock, I felt like I had a truckload of moldy manna from yesterday.

"It's like being Van Cliburn with his hands cut off," I told Joylene. "You still hear the music, but you can't play it."

During one such morning, a great sermon on Jesus and his disciples during the storm came to mind. I could visualize the introduction, the main points, the ending, everything. I could even hear the congregation laughing during the funny parts. If I closed my eyes, I could visualize the members sitting in their pews, nodding their heads in agreement as I shared and opened God's Word.

When I opened my eyes, I felt like a surface-to-air missile had pierced my heart. *That sermon will never be preached,* I thought. There is absolutely nothing more frustrating for a pastor than to come to such a realization. I felt like the butt of a practical joke gone bad.

The familiarity of Missouri had actually turned it into a haunting ground. I wanted to be with my friends, but I wanted to be with them as the "fun Duane," not as the "silent Duane." It didn't take much longer for Joylene to realize that even Missouri wouldn't work. We'd have to go farther, to a place where we knew fewer people. We'd visit my mother in Michigan.

## THE DEATH OF AUTUMN

Throughout my ordeal, my mother always maintained her faith, and at first it was an absolute joy to visit her. I still couldn't talk, but the pain was way down, so after spending a few days at her home, enjoying a vacation seemed possible. We had blown two, but three is a charm, right?

Northern Michigan is beautiful country and, like Missouri, has its share of good fishing. Consequently, the ladies in my life suggested that we go fishing "up north." Neither of them understand (nor do they intend to learn) any more about fishing than which end of the rod to hold, but they chatted away like excited children at the prospect. They finally convinced me to get some brochures and said they would take care of the reservations.

Since our income was Not Nearly at its previous level, we decided to stay in some less-than-four-star motels as we trekked to the north country. After all, we reasoned, this was a fishing trip, not a cruise. As we packed the van, we had no idea that this "fishing trip" would resemble Chevy Chase's *Vacation* movies.

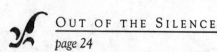

First stop was East Tawas, Michigan. Our conversation stopped dead as we pulled into the older motel where we had our reservations.

"Well," I said, trying to break the awkward silence, "it has a great view of Lake Huron."

Joylene added, "It seems *pretty* well kept."

Mother chimed in, "This will be fun."

It was a dive and we knew it, but we decided we were going to enjoy it anyway. I may have passed some uglier hotels, but I had certainly never slept in one.

We headed for the office to check in, and the reservation clerk greeted us warmly. "All right," she said, "one room for the Millers."

"Uh, that was *two* rooms," Joylene corrected her.

"*Two?*" the clerk asked. "I'm sorry, we must have lost one. I just have a reservation here for one room, and all the other rooms are booked with fishermen."

I couldn't believe that this motel would actually be able to put out a "No Vacancy" sign, but that was my first lesson that fishermen are far less discriminating than fish.

"Don't worry," the clerk perked up. "Your room is set up with two beds."

We looked at each other in disbelief, not sure what to do. I love my mother dearly, but I haven't slept in the same room with her for about forty-nine years! On the other hand, we weren't exactly in New York City. We were in East Tawas, Michigan, and our options were limited, at best.

Mother must have realized my discomfort because she started laughing and reminded me that she used to change my diapers. Surely, we could tolerate a common room for one night.

When we entered our room, sure enough there were two beds—one double and a rollaway. I told the gals that they could have the double and I would sleep on the rollaway. The only problem was that once I opened the rollaway, there was no space left in the room for walking.

*Duane Miller*

Have you ever seen a Three Stooges movie with Larry, Moe, and Curly in the same bed together? Well, that was the Miller clan on that first night. Duane and Bert on the outside and poor Joylene in the middle. ("For better or for worse," she had told the minister.) We really laughed (later) about having to turn in tandem during the night. And if anyone had needed to use the bathroom . . . well, forget it, it was out of the question.

Once we arrived at our final destination, Joylene knew that if she wanted to be near me, she'd have to sit in a fishing boat; so we went out on the lake together and I helped her prepare and cast her line.

Now, I've never debated the obvious fact that Joylene is better looking than me, and apparently the fish agreed too. Joylene's catch made mine look like a guppy.

"Okay, we can go home now," she said.

Her remark reminded me of the rookie poker player who gets lucky on the first hand and thinks the seasoned veterans are going to let him walk with their money!

"Not so fast," I said, but the bass apparently lost interest in feeding. My fish provided the appetizer that night, but Joylene's catch provided the main course.

After dinner, we sat in the living room of the cottage we had rented. "Duane," my mother said, "God's still gonna heal you. I believe that."

I appreciated what she was saying. I knew her heart was going out to her only son, and I loved her for her faith. At the same time, however, I felt that it was necessary that I be honest with her.

"I don't want to hear that, Mother. If He does, He does. I trust God and I know that nothing happens without His permission. But it's too discouraging to chase rainbows. I've got to deal with what is."

Though the pain in my throat had subsided somewhat, I had developed an ache in my soul that constantly sucked me down. It was a giant, emotional black hole that threatened to swallow my world. It never got my joy, but it took a big bite out of my happiness.

What do I mean by that? One of the lessons I've learned is that my joy isn't based on happiness, it's based on what is true. Happiness is a fleeting and wonderfully delightful emotion, but joy is the river that brings life to the forest. As I look back, I believe it's no coincidence that my wife's name is "Joylene." Hers was the steady love that nourished me when all the fleeting happy emotions lost their way.

To make matters more complicated, however, other physical problems developed while we were in Michigan. My equilibrium began to disappear. It was very frightening at first. Though it's not painful at all, losing your equilibrium completely distorts your sense of security. Suddenly, gravity becomes a sadistic ruler threatening to drop you at any moment. Joylene was forced to take my arm when we walked. Women do this all the time, but if someone looked closely he would see that rather than me supporting Joylene, she was supporting me.

Call me old-fashioned, but this bothered me.

I developed vision problems as well. My eyes would occasionally sting and go out of focus, and it would take several minutes for me to regain clarity of vision. I had already lost my speech. The thought of losing my sight made fear an ever present temptation.

But more than anything else, I hurt from being away from the people I loved in Brenham. You can take the pastor out of his church, but you can't take the church out of the pastor. I longed to be with my people, and I began inwardly counting the days until we could go home.

The Indian summer of our exile dissolved into autumn, and finally, the end of October arrived. Our six months were complete. Joylene and I repacked our bags, said goodbye to Galveston, Michigan, and Missouri—our three "vacations"—and headed back to Brenham.

## IF YOU DON'T KNOW, WHO DOES?

I wasn't a doctor, but I had gotten more than my share of experience as a patient. Because of this, my return was a frustrating and even somber event. Intuitively, I knew the six months' sabbatical hadn't done a thing for my voice; all I had to do was try to talk to know that. Joylene phoned the doctor to set up the next appointment, but I already knew what I was going to hear from him, and I really didn't want to hear it. I had left Brenham with sadness but great hope. The sadness hadn't gone, but reality had chipped away at the hope with every mile we drove back to Brenham.

Joylene was also nearing her end. She had now put up with my condition for almost a year, and certain aspects of our new life were grating on her like never before. Since I couldn't call to her when she was upstairs, I whistled for her. Well, we should have realized that there are few things more annoying than being whistled for. We didn't, and Joylene was afraid to tell me. She didn't want to hurt me anymore than I had already been hurt.

Consequently, Joylene might be in the middle of folding clothes upstairs or just relaxing, and my shrill whistle would pierce the air. One night, just before we went to the doctor, Joylene heard my whistle for the third time that day and just wanted to cry.

*Lord,* she prayed, *help me handle that whistle. I know there's no other way he can reach me. Help me be patient, please.*

Because our communication was so inhibited, mistakes of understanding became a common occurrence. For instance, we might be talking on the phone, and Joylene would misinterpret my written symbols and say something to the person on the other line that I didn't intend for her to say. I'd have to wave my hands to get her attention, then quickly try to write out a correction.

Not surprisingly, at times both of us became testy.

We went to the doctors on a Friday afternoon. I was desperate for good news—if six months didn't work, what would?—but reality hovered over me like a starving vulture. The doctors were upbeat when I walked in, and they asked me how my medicine—six months of "relaxation"—combatted the stress.

"Listen, doc," I croaked. "This six-month leave of absence might be good for some people, but it just doesn't work for pastors! We're people persons, and isolating us from our congregations aggravates the mental anguish. I might not have been stressed when I left, but I am now!"

My doctor smiled and said, "I'll take that under advisement."

And then we got serious.

Even after six months of rest, my voice was no different than it had been. The doctors compared a tape of my current voice with a tape that had been made six months earlier, and the tapes sounded identical.

After listening to the tapes, I looked at my lead physician and said, "It's no different, is it? Doc, talk to me. Give me a prognosis, some hope. What's going to happen? Where do we go from here?"

The doctor shook his head. "I don't know, Duane," he said. "I honestly don't know yet. We have a good bit more work to do."

*All right*, I thought, *it's time to get it out in the open.* I finally mustered the courage to ask the one burning question that had sat like an ignored elephant in the middle of our living room. "Then tell me this," I scratched out. "Will I ever get to preach again?"

His words hit me like a hungry hurricane: "I can't tell you one way or the other right now if you'll ever get better. I just don't know."

It's a good thing for that doctor that I didn't have any voice, because I wanted to shout, *"Well if you don't know, then who does?"*

We were talking about my life, my call, my wife's future, my kids' education. The church had been gracious enough to pay me a partial salary during my six-month stay, but that couldn't go on forever. And bills don't care whether you can talk or not. The mortgage company, the phone company, the grocer—everybody still wanted to be paid, and nobody gives discounts just because you've lost your voice.

Joylene and I shuffled back into the car. She offered no resistance when I told her that the time had come to resign my pastorate. It was inevitable, really, a heretofore unspoken assumption between us. My ministry was dead. Now it was time to bury it.

## THE FUNERAL

As soon as I got home, I set up a meeting with the deacon who was chairman of the personnel committee at our church. Steve is a Texas Ranger, and we sat in his police car at midnight as I told him about the doctor's current assessment.

"We need you, Duane," he said. "We need you to stay."

"I can't stay, Steve. I'm not physically able."

Steve turned away and looked out his window. How could he argue? "When do you plan to resign?" he asked.

"Sunday morning."

"You're kidding!"

I wasn't. It was now eleven months into my illness, and the congregation had been more than fair. They needed to deal with their challenges, and I needed to deal with mine. Unfortunately, that meant a parting of the ways.

I woke up on Sunday morning with a heavy heart. I had planned to die as pastor of the First Baptist Church in Brenham. In fact, when we had some sidewalk replaced in front of the church I had carved my name in the wet cement. I used to tease the congregation that my name was the only one in the church that was carved in stone. Leaving now felt like leaving in the middle of a sentence, but there was nothing I could do.

I walked into the church and asked the interim pastor if I could have the pulpit for a few minutes.

"Sure," he said. "What's up?"

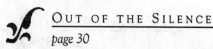

"I have to resign."

"You *can't* resign."

"I have to," I replied. "I'm not asking you, I'm telling you."

The congregation was silent as I stood up and walked to the microphone. It was the first time I had seen many of these people since we had left six months earlier. At first, a few faces were expectant and hopeful, but I saw some people in the front row flinch when I pulled the microphone so closely that it was pushing against my lips. I spoke as loudly and as concisely as I could.

"The doctors have told me there is no guarantee that I'll ever be able to preach again," I said. No use leading them on. "Y'all have been more than fair, but now—" I paused, it was still difficult to say, "now, you need a pastor. You can't hire one if I hang on. If there was any hope, if the doctors could give me the slightest possibility, I would stay. Without that assurance, I must step down."

As I left the pulpit, my soul was swirling with confusion. I had poured my heart and soul into this church for four years, but now I felt like a boy who sticks his hand in the bucket, swirls the water around, and then is forced to take it out. Moments later, there's absolutely no evidence that his hand was ever in the bucket. The church was certainly better off financially, but I was by no means done with my work there. Unresolved issues needed to be addressed, but they would have to be addressed by another pastor.

Because of my height—about 5-foot-6—and the fact that I've been small all my life, I've learned to be a fighter. I've never run from anything. When the high school varsity football coach told me I was too small to play, I filled my shoulder pads with determined sweat until I not only made the team but became a starting player. I've always felt I had something to prove, and leaving the job undone at Brenham was one of the hardest things I've ever had to do.

My resignation was more than an announcement. It was a funeral service for my dreams. God had obviously redirected my journey, and this stretch resembled nothing as much as a long, dark tunnel with a twist in the middle that blocked even the point of light at the end.

That afternoon the kids came home from college, and we sat around and visited. The doctors had lifted my speaking ban, but it was still very difficult to communicate. Sadness pervaded the air like heavy humidity on a hot summer day.

The next morning, Joylene and I went to my office and packed up four years' worth of labor. We boxed up my books, gathered my personal belongings, and loaded the van. I paused for a moment before I turned out the light. I just wanted to get a last look. With a sigh of resignation, I flicked off the switch and closed the door.

*Well,* I thought, *this chapter is over. Where will the next one begin?*

# chapter four

# Sorrow
and
Love

FOR THE FIRST TIME IN MY ADULT LIFE, I woke up the next morning without a job. Everything I have ever done in life to earn a living—from sales to ministry to being a professional singer—has been related to my ability to communicate. My hands are pretty much useless unless they're gesturing in a sermon. The thought of retraining at my age and doing something mechanical not only didn't seem practical, but to those who knew me, it seemed absurd.

As I considered my vocational options, I looked at my hands and winced, remembering the time our daughter Jodi had a minor fender bender. Dave Tinker, a wonderful friend and member of our former Sunday school class, had told me that getting a dent out of a car is really no problem. He lent me a tool and told me how to use it.

"It's real easy," I remember him saying. He was a man of integrity, and I had no reason to doubt him. I soon learned, however, that there are different definitions of "easy."

The contraption that he lent me had a bolt that you screw into the dent. Once it's in, you gently pull it back, and the dent disappears.

That's the way it's supposed to work, anyway. When I tried it, I somehow stripped out the hole, leaving the dent and creating an even bigger hole, a hole that putty couldn't fill, at least not with my level of expertise.

Now, not only did Jodi still have a dent, she had a hole, which eventually rusted out and proved to everybody in our community that her father was all thumbs and no forefingers when it came to anything mechanical.

Ask my wife or either of my daughters, and they'll tell you: I'm world famous for turning an oil change into a three-hundred-dollar repair bill. It's gotten to the point where both of my daughters try to hide anything that's wrong with their cars because, naturally, I believe in miracles, and one of these days I believe I can get a broken-down car back on the road. My daughters are a bit more skeptical. Whenever I get that twinkle in my eye, I hear them plead, "Please, Daddy, don't fix it."

With these hands, how in the world was I going to make a living? I had two daughters in college, a wife who had been out of the job market for over fifteen years, and—with the absence of my voice—no marketable job skills. There was literally nothing for me to do in Brenham if I couldn't pastor, so the decision to move back to Houston was virtually automatic.

But how to get back?

I have to digress a bit to tell you about the *second* miracle in this book (actually, there are dozens, as you'll soon see), and that's a group called "the Catacombs class" at First Baptist Church in Houston, Texas. I was on staff with the church in Houston immediately prior to my stint at Brenham, and the Catacombs Sunday school class was literally a church within a church. First Baptist in Houston has twenty-thousand-plus members, so you can fit a lot of congregations within that one church!

I had taught the Catacombs class for years, and when I accepted the senior pastorate at Brenham in 1986, it meant resigning not only from my position as staff member at Houston First Baptist but also as teacher of the Catacombs class. This was by no means an automatic or even easy decision. I was perfectly content to remain an associate pastor at First Baptist. Dr. John Bisagno, the senior pastor, and I had prayed about my leaving for over a year. Finally, one day Brother John told me, "Look, Duane, I can't keep you here. You're too good a preacher. It's not fair to the body of Christ."

Shortly thereafter, Joylene and I decided to accept the position at Brenham. We did so fully believing that Brenham was God's will for us at the time, and there was plenty of anticipation and excitement about the new challenges I would face while serving as a senior pastor. Our excitement over the future was tempered, however, by what we were leaving behind. You don't shut the door on love like we had in Houston without having second, third, or even fourth thoughts.

The Catacombs class was determined not to make it any easier on me. On my first Sunday as pastor at Brenham, I was caught up in the excitement that always greets the arrival of a new pastor. I was shaking hands, doing my best to burn names and faces into my memory, and eager to deliver a good first sermon. When I stepped into the pulpit and looked out into the congregation for the first time, I was startled to see about thirty members from my Catacombs class sitting in the front pews. I could imagine that a few might come, but thirty?

I remember thinking, *I hope these guys behave themselves or I'm gonna get off to a rocky start.*

Well, before I could even complete my thoughts, the thirty members unfurled a huge sign, which they had hung over a rail so that it would be visible to just me and the choir. The sign read:

"Love You? YES! Forgive You? NEVER!"

Where did such love come from? Prior to 1986, the Catacombs class stuck together like ants at a picnic. Life had literally knit our hearts to each other. Together we had placed parents in nursing homes; helped families cope with suicide; placed children in detox centers; and lovingly confronted wayward husbands, saying, "Yes, you're going to leave that girl-friend, and yes, you're going back to your wife."

It's not that the class *planned* to be so helpful. More often than not, the generous acts were spontaneous. Because the class was so large, resources were plentiful. If someone had to move, two dozen people were ready to help at a moment's notice. If a relative was getting out of prison, somebody would have access to a car and a reference for a job. One time, we even helped a class member to network with a former cult member so that a daughter could be persuaded to leave a cult!

From cutting hair at downtown missions to serving dinners to hungry people, the Catacombs class had played together, laughed together, cried together, worshiped together, and studied God's Word together. Cherie Young, codirector of the class with her husband, Robert, had grown used to members pressing cash into her hand after or before the class and whispering, "Give this to so-and-so. I've heard he just lost his job."

Leaving the Catacombs class had been one of the hardest things I'd ever done. Even after several years, being away from those folks made us feel like a part of us was missing. You know, there are plenty of churches that claim miracles happening all the time. There are more congregations than I can count that have a crackerjack preacher who can parse Greek and make even the book of Revelation sound sensible. But one of the things that makes First Baptist of Houston stand out is that it is a church that has plumbed the depths of love. It knows what love is, how love applies, and how love regenerates the despairing, hurting, and downcast.

On the lonely Saturday of our departure from Brenham, Joylene and I had a taste of that love. We were sipping our morning cups of coffee in preparation for loading up the truck and moving back to Houston. Joylene looked disbelieving at me when our doorbell rang at 7 A.M.

"Who'd be calling at this hour?" Joylene wanted to know.

I shrugged my shoulders and went to answer the door. When I opened it, I saw the people who meant more than the world to me.

"We understand you're moving!" one of them laughed and shouted. I cried. There were the Youngs, directors of the Catacombs class; the Wilsons, who lent us their house in Galveston; the Lopezes, the unofficial "huggers and greeters" of the Catacombs class; the Smiths, the Jordans, the Balls, the Walkers, and others. I've never seen faces look so beautiful in all my life.

They came with their bodies, their trucks, and their love to help a hurting, defeated couple in the midst of their grief. We weren't their pastors anymore; we weren't their teachers; we weren't even members of their church (our membership had been transferred to Brenham). But love breaks all bounds, and the Catacombs class broke several that day.

At one of the lowest points in our life, when we felt lonely and afraid, we were reminded that, as far as the Catacombs class was concerned, we would never be alone. We had entered a season of chaos, but the Catacombs class became our point of sanity.

## RETRIEVED

Coming home to Houston felt like being enveloped in a warm, cushy hug. We went to the Catacombs class the very next day, and Cherie Young stood up and announced, "We went to Brenham yesterday and retrieved the Millers."

Have you ever had one of those moments when God lets you know through someone else that He knows how you're feeling? Someone uses a phrase, a choice of words, or a description, and you think, *That's not an accident. That's God.*

That's what happened to me when Cherie said, "We went to Brenham yesterday and retrieved the Millers." The class clapped and yelled, and my darkened soul felt a piercing light for the first time in months as I heard Cherie say that word, *retrieved.* God knew how desperately I needed to hear that I had

*Duane Miller*

been brought back to a place where I was loved and needed and missed. In the midst of my pain, I sat in that beautiful chapel surrounded by the world's most beautiful people and thought, maybe, just maybe, God really does have a plan for my life after all.

God fit an entire sermon into that one word. He electrified my mind and startled my awareness with the deep truths imbedded in its use.

*Retrieved* . . .

I had been brought home.

*Retrieved* . . .

I had been missed.

*Retrieved* . . .

I was still needed.

That word lifted my spirits in the following days, especially as I considered once again our increasingly limited vocational options.

Our finances were a mess. The church in Brenham had managed to pay me a half-salary while I was on sabbatical, and some dear friends had helped with generous gifts during the year. Additionally, by this time I was receiving some disability income from a policy we had purchased, but I had not received a full salary in almost a year. My bills for medical care, the "enforced vacation," deposits for utilities, housing, and so forth, all had left us tapped. I had two daughters attending Baylor University, and the doctors could give me no hope—or even a good guess—about my future prognosis. The questions were as endless as the answers were elusive, but knowing that I had been retrieved, and knowing that I was loved, helped to make all the unanswered questions bearable.

As soon as we were tucked into a condominium in Houston, the Catacombs class began doing what I call "knotting up around us." They tied themselves around us as a support system, loving us, praying for us, doing all those things that lonely and hurting people need done for them. Sometimes, a member would just drop by and invite us to lunch. It was such a simple gesture, but to us it meant, "You still matter. People still care about you."

Other class members left messages on our answering machine: "Duane, I know you can't talk, but we just wanted you to know that we love you and are praying for you." Some stopped by for unexpected visits and made sure we knew that we were still considered valuable and indispensable members of the community, even if I could no longer serve that community as a teacher.

In short, they lived Romans 12:15: "Rejoice with those who rejoice, and weep with those who weep."

The absolutely beautiful part about all this—the part that, even now, still brings tears to my eyes—is that none of it was orchestrated. Not once did Cherie get up in front of the class and say, "Now people, you know the Millers are facing a difficult time. Let's pass a list around the room and see who can make phone calls, who can fix a meal, and who can pay them a visit."

That didn't happen. People responded spontaneously and on their own, but together they became a lovely symphony of support in the midst of our silence.

A few months after we came back, we returned to the beach house in Galveston, only this time, we weren't alone. A number of Catacombs class members went down to prepare for the annual Catacombs class crawfish boil. About one hundred people usually showed up, and together we'd consume about three to four hundred pounds of crawfish (the ocean went down an inch when the Catacombs class came to town!). The night before, about twenty of us went down early—ostensibly to make preparations but mostly to have a good time. We made sure the coffee was hot for the members as they arrived the next morning, but outside of that, most of the time was spent telling stories, laughing, and enjoying the good fellowship.

That night, however, as we sat around talking and sharing and praying about my situation, the mood turned sober. Several people told me stories about what my teaching ministry had meant to them. This helped me to understand that Joylene and I weren't the only ones feeling the pain of my illness. Other people were suffering too, and though that realization didn't restore my voice, it did help to defeat some of the loneliness that had begun to develop.

Muril Wilson told me, "Duane, I know this isn't over yet."

One of the things I love about this group is that they are realists. None of us felt like we had to manufacture faith; nobody was phony. We were free to utter sentences like, "I don't understand what's going on, but this can't be the end."

The more we talked, though, the more nothing made any sense. There just didn't seem to be any answers, and soon, every eye was wet with tears. You couldn't have found a dry Kleenex in the house by the time we were through.

I faced the indignity of more medical tests, the humiliation of being without a viable vocational future, and the anguish of watching my singing and preaching ministry being completely shut down, but I no longer faced these things alone. There were so many unknowns, but each one of these unknowns was tempered by the knowledge that they would be faced together, and not just with Joylene, but with the entire Catacombs class behind me.

I had held their hands on so many occasions. Now it was my turn to be in the center and to serve as the object of everyone's concern. It's not a role I would have chosen. It certainly wasn't one I had aspired to. But it brought such a strength into my soul that I honestly don't know how I would have made it otherwise.

## THE LANGUAGE OF THE SPIRIT

Lurking financial disaster forced Joylene and me to mention the unmentionable: Joylene getting a job. At first glance, this might not seem like such a challenge. Joylene is by no means a shy, retiring flower. She grew up in Africa as a missionary kid, serving several stints at boarding school, and learned to be self-reliant. She is strong and capable and has an unshak-

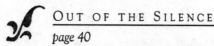

able faith. But she had been out of the workforce for over fifteen years and really had no desire to go back into it. All of a sudden, however, her husband was unemployed and, for the moment, apparently unemployable. We had to start considering other options.

This rocked my faith like few things ever have. I've always worked, even from the time I was a small boy. Throughout most of my childhood and adolescence, my dad was the vice president and general manager of a large paint, wallpaper, and floor-covering firm. He had dropped out of high school during the Depression, as so many others had done, in order to help his mother feed three hungry boys. Since he had worked so hard to achieve what he had done, he took the "work ethic" very seriously.

I found out just *how* seriously when I went to work for him. He expected me to work harder than anyone else. Some people might have thought that the boss's son would have gotten extra slack, but the opposite was true. My dad made it clear to me that it was my responsibility to set an example.

I remember one time, after we had just finished unloading and stocking some paint, and there were no customers in the store, I gave my feet a needed break and sat down on some cans of paint.

My dad walked into the store and saw me sitting down. I flinched when I saw the jaw muscles literally weave knots around his mouth as they tightened.

"Duane," he said, "I need to speak with you. *Now.*"

I hopped off the cans and followed him into his office. "I don't *ever* want to catch you sitting down again. You understand me?"

"But, Dad," I protested, "everybody else takes a break when we finish unloading a truck. There wasn't anything else to do right then."

"Then pick up a broom and start sweeping."

His tone was such that I didn't dare argue.

*Duane Miller*

With that background, it was particularly difficult for me to face the prospect of being supported by my wife. Conceivably I could have done some sort of menial labor, so long as it didn't include the use of my voice. But do you realize how many jobs require just that? I had been a salesman years earlier, but now if I tried to communicate over the phone, I was likely to be mistaken for an obscene caller! Would *you* give your credit card number or make an appointment with a man who sounded like a hoarse Marlon Brando in *The Godfather*?

I shudder—literally—when I think back upon those days, but you know what? Now, I wouldn't give them up. God used that pit experience to open my eyes to many new realities. Just recently, for instance, I was talking to a group of black pastors, and I gained an entirely new understanding of what it's like to be discriminated against.

"For the first time in my life," I told them, "I felt utterly useless. My income, my future, my health, my sense of well-being, all were suddenly beyond my control. It was a terrifying and humbling experience."

I looked up and was caught short. As I looked into the eyes of these precious men of God, *I knew they knew.* They understood in a way that many of my other friends and associates couldn't.

It's often said that experience is the best teacher. I didn't want to hear it back then, but now I see its truth. It was only after I experienced such pain and futility that I could really understand what others have to go through. Let's face it. A healthy white male has opportunities that others do not. My socioeconomic background and education gave me a start that some members of various minorities have never experienced. Lack of education, lack of experience, lack of contacts—or just plain old ugly prejudice or racism—can mercilessly slam doors shut when people seek to secure gainful employment. Sure, there are always some who are able to break through, but are we willing to empathize with someone who is tired of having his nose smashed by yet another slamming door; who just can't bear to be told one more time, "Sorry, you're just not good enough. We've decided to hire someone else"?

Now, when I hear of someone who's just gotten out of jail, who has no job, no skills, no car, and no place to live—well, I know how that person feels. I've tasted the hopelessness. I've felt the anger, frustration, and tension swirling in my stomach.

Not that long ago, I spoke with a young man, "Ricky," who was in prison. He was twenty-eight and black, and he said something that both startled me and reminded me of the weary resignation I once wore. I had tried to comfort him by saying, "Well, it's almost over now. It won't be that much longer until you're out." But he shook me by saying, "Oh, I'll be back."

His tone was so matter-of-fact that I could scarcely believe what I was hearing. "You'll what?" I asked.

"I'll be back."

I knew he hated prison. I could see the distress in his eyes, so I said, "I don't understand that. Does that mean you like it here?"

He laughed. "No, I don't like it here, but I'll be back."

"If you don't like it here," I asked, "and you've been through all this—" I stretched my arms out toward the prison walls, "and you know what it's like, then why in the world would you do something to get back?"

Ricky looked at me with eyes that were deadly serious. "Well, let's look at it like this," he said. "I'm black, I'm a high school dropout and in truth can barely read and write, I have no job skills, and I'm an ex-con. Are you gonna hire me?"

All at once I understood. He felt hopeless, and in all honesty, he had little reason to feel any other way. The chances of his finding a decent job that paid enough to support his family were lodged somewhere between slim and none. Ricky was experienced enough to realize that eventually he'd feel forced back into selling drugs and that eventually (it was only a matter of time) he'd be caught again. And that meant he'd be right back where he started, hating the drudgery of each day spent in a crowded prison cell with other beaten-down individuals.

*Duane Miller*

He didn't like it. He didn't want it to be that way, but as he took an honest look at his life, he couldn't see a realistic alternative.

Because of my experience, I was able to understand Ricky rather than judge him. I've worn the clouded lenses of hopelessness, I know what they do to a man's vision, and I kept my religious clichés and platitudes tucked safely inside my briefcase. Ricky deserved much more than that.

Today, I don't attempt to have the answers. I've learned the power of hugs and even tears, both of which often speak a far more effective message than words. Words come cheap, and they penetrate the ears. Hugs and tears are the currency of the soul, and they penetrate the spirit. Speaking this language represents the biggest change in my personality that has resulted from my three-year ordeal.

## GOD PROVIDES GOD'S WAY

*So God*, I prayed, *I'm learning a valuable lesson, but how do I pay for my daughters' tuition?*

I remembered years back, when I was in Bible school, and I met a fellow classmate from the drug-infested streets of New York. He had met the Lord and felt called to train for the ministry, even though he had no help—financial or otherwise—from his family. When he arrived at our Bible college, he was never sure from one month to the next where his tuition and money for other expenses was going to come from.

"Got your payment yet, Paul?" I remember asking him, just days before the deadline.

"Not yet," he'd say and smile. "But God will provide."

Sure enough, the afternoon the payments were due, I'd walk by and see Paul wearing a smile that could put Mary Lou Retton to shame.

"God provides, Duane!" he'd say.

I never had that experience. Not once did unexpected funds show up in my mailbox. In fact, I remember praying, *How*

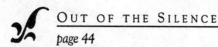

*come, God? Why him and not me? I never get any unexpected checks. I always have to work to pay my way. What's the deal?*

Over time, the "deal" became very clear. Paul had grown up on the streets; he had no background in the church, in the Scriptures, or any of the things of God. On the other hand, I had had a "drug" problem since I was a baby. My parents drug me to Sunday school, they drug me to morning worship, and if the doors of the church were open during the middle of the week, they drug me to that meeting as well.

Many of the things Paul was learning and struggling to learn, I had known for most of my life. He would not have had time to work and study, so the Lord provided him with the opportunity to focus 100 percent on this radical new thing called the Christian life.

On the other hand, God gave me the opportunity to use my "spare time" profitably and thereby provided for me as well. I had taken it for granted, but now I realized that God provides in different ways. One of those ways is spelled J-O-B.

Well, it was one thing for God to provide by giving me a job. It was quite another for God to provide by providing my *wife* with a job. I wasn't at all ready to experience that.

## ROLE REVERSAL

When the unmentionable became inevitable, Joylene sat down and began to write her first resume in almost two decades. I can't describe how terrifying this was for her. It was difficult for her because it meant she'd have to face down the demons of her childhood.

Joylene had the best parents any girl could hope for. They had pastored churches in rural Nebraska before itinerating and going to Africa as full-time missionaries. Being a preacher's kid is not an easy thing, however, no matter how terrific your parents may be. Living in a "glass house" where your every action is known and can affect your father's career, moving more often than most people do and therefore not forming strong and lasting childhood friendships, and ultimately, finding yourself in a foreign country where you were never "called" to go, all contribute to some serious insecurities. Add to that the experience of being teased about your "funny" accent at the first school you attend after leaving America (a British school), and an eight-year-young lady subconsciously begins to feel that she will never "fit in."

When I reminisce about a high school homecoming game, Joylene can't really relate. The kids she grew up with are now scattered all over the world. She doesn't have a single buddy-type friendship that goes back to childhood. Consequently, she has always felt a bit like the "odd man out" when I get together with my childhood chums and discuss "the good old days."

It was perhaps inevitable that such an upbringing would result in a certain insecurity, particularly in the workplace. And since Joylene doubted her own abilities, how could she sell others on them? You see, the very skills she would need to secure employment were the skills she felt she lacked most.

Though she did have something to fall back on—Joylene trained as an X-ray technologist before we were married—it had been more than fifteen years since she had practiced in that profession. It might as well have been a hundred years, considering the technical advances that are made in such a profession.

Our daughters were fabulous, and they relished the role reversal as they helped their mother try to land a new job. They read over her resume, suggested changes, told her what style was "in," and gave her tips for interviews.

Joylene's initial inclination was to find something in a field other than X-ray. She feared that she had fallen too far behind ever to catch up and thought it might be easier to start fresh. As she tested the job market and reviewed her options, however, she reluctantly came to the conclusion that a job as an X-ray technologist would provide her with the best opportunity.

Now, keep in mind that Houston is *not* some backwoods medical city. As I mentioned before, the diverse facilities of Houston draw the brightest and the best. Joylene, with her fifteen-year-old resume, had to compete with technicians who were on the cutting edge of their profession.

There is a God, however, and Joylene found some doctors who were willing to take a chance on her. I was so proud of her for putting herself in that position and mustering the strength to show she could do the job—even when she wasn't sure if she really could.

I'll not soon forget the first morning Joylene left for work. I had very mixed emotions. I was grateful to God that He had provided a source of income, but at the same time I felt terrible that it wasn't coming through me. It was a bitter pill to be the dependent.

Joylene was anxious but brave as we kissed at the door. As soon as the door shut, tears washed down my face. Joylene's leaving for work became a personal picture of what I had become—or maybe, more appropriately, of what I had lost.

*This is not the way I planned my life,* I thought. *This is not the way I was raised.* And then, this thought stung even more: *My daddy would not be proud of this.*

I had become all too familiar with tears, and now was no exception. But even in that sorrow, I found some joy. I was so grateful and proud of Joylene. She had faced her fears, stepped out of her comfort zone, and pitched in when I needed her.

I was reminded of that hymn: "Sorrow and love flow mingled down." That's how I was feeling—an intense sadness at the way things were, but an intense love, appreciation, and joy for Joylene.

I stopped crying and started praying. "God," I prayed, "give Joylene courage. Help her to face her fears. She hasn't worked in fifteen years, and she's scared to death. Be her comfort."

A silent voice told me that this job would be initially uncomfortable and even scary for Joylene, but that in the long run, it was part of God's plan to help Joylene become the woman God had created her to be. Since she was in her early forties, some might have called Joylene "middle-aged." But that morning, my pain was tempered when I realized that in God's hand, Joylene was just a bud, and under His watchful care, she was about to bloom.

I had to admit, it was a miracle that Joylene had gotten the job in the first place. But God knew our financial situation needed Joylene to have a good job so we could pay the bills. And God also knew that Joylene needed this job so that she could become the strong woman He had in mind.

# Desert Flowers

THERE ARE FEW THINGS IN THIS world more remarkable than desert flowers. When people think of deserts, they think of vast, uninterrupted expanses of hot, blowing sand. But here and there God has planted the delicacy, beauty, and irony of a desert flower.

Though God often asks His people to walk through many deserts, He occasionally graces their journey with a fragrant flower. In the coming months, Joylene and I would hold onto these brief reprieves and learn to enjoy them as long as they would last.

The first such "desert flower" was the change wrought in Joylene. I may have lost my voice, but I gained a new wife.

Joylene succeeded fabulously at her new job. (As far as we know, there are only three people in Houston who glow in the dark!) She became stronger and more self-assured. She was also more patient. Being at work for eight hours a day was like therapy for her. She was able to absorb herself in something else and forget about me for a while, and it did wonders for her soul and our marriage. When Joylene came home, she was physically tired, of course, but emotionally ready to face the challenge of living with a husband who couldn't speak.

Joylene began to feel more "a part of the team" than she ever had before. In a way, my strengths had kept her strengths hidden. Now, she was rising to the challenge and loving it.

Even today, I'm thankful for what that challenge did to our marriage. God was able to take a humbling situation and use it to build Joylene's confidence and confront my pride.

Five years ago, if Joylene wanted to go shopping, she'd say, "Duane, what do you think? Should I go to the store and get this now, or wait? Or do you want to come with me?"

When she asked this, she was making sure her actions wouldn't inconvenience or upset me. Inadvertently, however, she had made me her point of reference. I was her "plumb line" against which all her activities and plans had to be measured.

Today, I'll hear something like this: "Duane, I need to go to the mall and get some shoes. I'll be back by nine o'clock."

While some husbands might be threatened by this, I like it. Joylene has shown me that she can survive without me. It would be difficult, as it would be for most anyone who loses a spouse, but she could make it. Knowing this has given me a new respect for her, which has strengthened the foundation of our marriage and helped us to seek new depths of intimacy.

Joylene's strength has affected other aspects of her life as well. When Joylene first started working for her new employer, she was emotionally tied to the technician's manual, almost in the same way that a toddler is tied to a comfort blanket. If she couldn't find that manual for half an hour, she'd start to panic, because without the manual, she'd have to make do on her own—and nothing scared Joylene as much as depending on herself.

Today, it would take Joylene hours to locate the technician's manual, but she doesn't care because she doesn't need it. She's learned that God has created her to be a very capable woman.

Let me give one other example. Because of her soft and kind personality, Joylene used to let people run over her. She never fought back, and in fact she rarely even spoke up.

Instead, she'd take all the abuse and suffer for days internally as the tension worked its way through her body. A few months ago, however, one of the attending physicians at the hospital really let her have it in a situation that unfairly implicated Joylene.

I was shocked when, a few days later, Joylene came home and told me, "By the way, I talked to Dr. —."

"Really?" I asked, my interest piqued.

"Yes. I told him I didn't appreciate the way I'd been treated."

I was stunned. For years I had preached eloquent lectures about how Joylene should stand up for herself, but none of them took hold. Within months of me losing my voice, Joylene began doing just that.

It was an adjustment for me when I realized Joylene no longer "needed" me to the extent that she did before; but I think that's healthy, that's good, and I'm thrilled for her.

Some married couples can only wonder how a partner would react if a major crisis came along. I don't have to wonder. I know. When Joylene and I stood before the altar and promised to stick together for better or worse, in sickness and in health, until death do us part, that was more than a civil ceremony, that was a holy commitment—a commitment made to each other and to God. Now, I know that I know that I know that she meant it!

On one occasion, I asked Joylene how she was managing all the change in her life. "Why are you doing this?" I asked. If she had just gotten rid of me, she could have removed 90 percent of the stress in her life.

"Duane," she said, "you'd do the same thing for me. Why wouldn't I do it for you?"

And Joylene still did everything possible to maintain what little ego I had left. She understood how tender I had become and how emasculated I had begun to feel. When a couple suggested going out to dinner, Joylene would take the wife aside and say, "Now, what did you have in mind?"

The other wife would make a suggestion, and Joylene would rate it on its atmosphere. We had learned that some restaurants were simply too loud for me to participate in the conversation. With booming background music, it would be impossible for me to be heard. If the couple had thought about such a restaurant, Joylene would make an alternate suggestion. She didn't want me to end up in a situation where my disability would be emphasized.

She found other ways to protect me as well. Over the Christmas holidays, when my daughters were home from college, I stepped outside to hang Christmas lights on the roof. Lisa and Jodi came out and talked to me the entire time. I remember thinking how considerate it was of them to keep their old man company while I climbed up the ladder and walked along the roof. It wasn't until after my experience was over that I learned Joylene had sent them out to be with me in case I fell, knowing that in such a circumstance I would have been unable to call for help.

I can't tell you how much it meant to my spirit that Joylene continued to show me all the love and respect she had shown before my illness. She had loved and appreciated me when I was able to provide for the family and we were financially comfortable, and she loved and appreciated me just as much when she was the one providing financially and "budget adjustments" were a regular occurrence.

## FINANCIAL FOLLIES

While Joylene's employment took the edge off our financial crisis, it by no means overcame it. Remember, we not only had two children in college, we had medical expenses as well. Though we did our best to keep up our faith, money became a *major* issue. When couples tell me they feel hopeless before the mounting bills, it's easy for me to empathize.

One afternoon, I experienced a particularly painful blow. I was walking down the stairs when I overheard a conversation between Joylene and our daughters. The girls had come home from college, ostensibly to visit; but as I approached unheard, I listened to them ask Joylene, "What should we do? Should we drop out of school?"

I wanted to drop to my knees, it hurt so bad, but I'll never forget Joylene's response as I quickly backed up. With a settled faith and a determined voice, she said, "Girls, I don't understand what God is doing right now, but this one thing I do know: He did not bring us into the desert to kill us. He will make a way for us. *Stay in school.*"

Financially, my girls have seen it all. Before I went into the ministry full-time, I ran a successful insurance business and was even able to buy my own plane. Our daughters enjoyed the benefits of a country club membership—tennis, swim team, the works.

I then mixed business interests with a fellow about whom I had been warned but who I was sure would act differently with me. Unfortunately, one of his positive traits was consistency, and soon my family and I were staring into the black hole of bankruptcy.

We learned back then how to trade Starbucks coffee for store-brand versions and how to suspend all magazine subscriptions and stay up late to make cheaper long-distance phone calls. Now, we were back to that don't-spend-anything-unless-you-absolutely-have-to stage.

The difficult part of financial duress is that everything becomes a conscious decision. It becomes exhausting. On one occasion Joylene and I were walking through the grocery store, and I instinctively reached out and picked up half a gallon of Blue Bell ice cream. Before I dropped it into the basket, however, I thought, *Can we really afford this? Is this essential?*

We had already put back all the fun stuff that masquerades as food—potato chips, soda, that type of thing. But Blue Bell ice cream! Did we have to go that far?

I dropped the carton of ice cream back into the freezer, realizing that I'd feel guilty anytime I took a bite of it anyway. Might as well leave it in the store.

*Duane Miller*

We dropped cable. We stopped going out to eat. We didn't buy new clothes for four years. We turned the air conditioning on eighty (remember, this is Houston!). Before we took a trip, we calculated what the gasoline would cost us.

Nothing is easy when you're broke. You can't turn on a light or run the water without thinking, *Can I afford this?*

It's no fun, believe me.

Many nights I'd lie awake in bed, staring at the ceiling. I'd get up, wearing frustration more tightly than my pajamas, and go downstairs to pray and think. Though the overall prayer—deliverance and healing—wasn't immediately answered, an answer to an individual prayer—about where we would live—startled me with God's generosity.

## THE BEST CHRISTMAS PRESENT OF ALL

The one-bedroom condo we moved into when we returned to Houston was fine for a night or two, but after several weeks it was extremely confining. We had to find a permanent address, preferably one near Joylene's work. Hours and then days were consumed as we crossed and recrossed Houston, searching for a home in a good location that was priced within our range. Remember, our finances were so tight we were still leaving Blue Bell ice cream in the store.

Houston is no different than most communities. You can virtually establish the price of a home by determining how far the commute would be. Joylene worked in the heart of the medical center, where doctors and their staff pulled down hundreds of thousands (or even millions) of dollars a year (most of them deserving every penny they get).

Still, we needed a place to live, and on Christmas Eve morning, I spotted a tiny little ad in the paper for a home just a few miles from where Joylene now worked and where I spent so much of my time. There was no price listed on the house in the ad, but from its location, I had a pretty good idea of what they would be asking, and it wouldn't be anywhere near what we could pay. Even though I was sure it would be priced well beyond our reach, we decided to give it a try.

Joylene and the girls (who were home for the holidays) started bubbling as soon as I read them the description of the house.

"Don't get too excited," I warned them. "This house probably costs far more than we could ever afford. Besides," I added, "it's Christmas Eve. I doubt we can even find someone who is willing to show it to us."

I called the number and, much to my surprise, the man who answered it said he'd be delighted to show us the house. Joylene and I, along with our daughters and my mother (who had come down from Michigan for a visit), piled into our minivan and drove over to the house.

"It sounds so perfect," my mother said.

"It'd be great for Mom," Lisa said. "She wouldn't have to drive so far."

"I can't wait!" Jodi chimed in.

"Now remember," I warned, not wanting to play the role of the Grinch on Christmas Eve, "it won't do to get overly excited. Even if we like the house—which we haven't even seen—it's unlikely we can afford it."

My speech had great effect—for about half a second. The women were excited, and the last thing they needed or wanted was a downbeat dad!

We pulled up to the house and saw how well it had been maintained. The soft-toned color was perfect for us, the street looked welcoming, and everybody but me wanted to rush into the door right that instant and say, "We'll take it!"

"Shhhh!" I said, trying to quiet everybody down. "Don't be too eager. I can't make an offer if you look too enthusiastic."

The man opened the door, and my wife, kids, and mother immediately began talking about where they could put the furniture.

*Duane Miller*

"Oh, Mom," one of the girls said, "this wall would be perfect for your zebra skin." (My wife's stint as a missionary kid in Africa has left us with a good number of game trophies.)

"Yes, and you could put the couch there, right against that wall," my mother added.

"This room is great!"

"Hey, let's go see what our bedrooms look like!"

I covered my eyes with my hands as I realized all attempts at posturing had been blown completely out of the water. This guy knew we wanted the house; I could imagine him adding hundreds or even thousands to the asking price on the spot.

We walked up the stairs.

"This one's mine!"

"Oh, look in here! I'm gonna love it!"

Obviously, my family had seen enough. The man and I walked downstairs while the women mentally decorated the top floor.

I took a deep breath. "How much are you asking?"

The man's reply felt like a sudden eclipse. The amount he mentioned was entirely out of our range. I knew I'd have to go upstairs and be the bearer of bad news. *Sorry kids, sorry Joylene, we just can't afford it.* They would understand—I was certain of that—but I was growing weary of disappointing them.

The man read my face. "Is that too much?" he asked.

"I'm sorry. We just can't give you anywhere near that amount," I said in my raspy voice, and started to walk back upstairs. *Better to get the bad news over with now before my family starts decorating the bathroom,* I thought. It was about the only room they hadn't discussed yet.

"Well, how much can you afford?"

I turned around, too embarrassed to speak. We had no business even looking at this house. I should have known it all along. We had bothered this man the day before Christmas, for crying out loud.

Still, he wanted to know, so I took a deep breath and offered about 40 percent of his asking price, then braced myself for his laugh or, even worse, anger. *You brought me out here on Christmas Eve when that's all you could afford? The nerve of it! Who do you think you are!*

Instead, the man held out his hand and said, "I'll take it."

My mouth dropped open, and I almost fell to my knees. I wouldn't have been more surprised if he had sprouted wings and started flying around the room!

"You'll—you'll take it?"

His smile was wide, and his handshake was firm. This wasn't a joke. This was really happening!

Talk about a Christmas present! In a tight housing market, in the midst of one of Houston's most desirable areas with property at a premium, we had just made a deal on a house that, logically speaking, we shouldn't even have been looking at. A realtor would surely have steered us away from even entering the door.

The women were ecstatic when I told them the good news. We never dreamed we'd find such a place.

It was Christmas, and I couldn't help but think of the familiar Christmas verse from Isaiah 9:2:

*The people who walked in darkness*
*Have seen a great light;*
*Those who dwelt in the land of the shadow of death,*
*Upon them a light has shined.*

We felt like we were living in the land of the shadow of death, but God sent a light to pierce our darkness. Joylene was so happy she wept. It wasn't just the home; it was the spiritual significance behind it. The miraculous way in which we received this dwelling spoke to our spirits just when we needed to hear God's voice the most.

God's grace was so evident. He knew the strain on Joylene—wanting to keep the girls in college, fighting to pay the bills, coping with her husband's illness, facing the challenges of a new job—and this was His way of saying, "I haven't forgotten you. I want you to know I love you. Sometimes you have to swallow a bitter pill, but here's a Snickers bar. Enjoy it."

A "new" wife and a new home were the first two "desert flowers" that I experienced. God had yet a third to send my way, however.

## WORK!

Just a few weeks later, a member of Houston's First Baptist Church and a dear friend, W. T. Smith, gave me a call. W. T. and the other members of the class had been praying for me to find some type of employment that didn't require the use of my voice. I went to his office, eager to hear what he had to say.

"Duane," he told me, "I think I've found something for you."

"Tell me." I wanted to know.

"We've got a contract with a federal agency here in Houston. Ever hear of the savings and loan crisis?"

I chuckled. At the time, it was the only thing the media was talking about. "Sure," I replied.

"Well, this federal agency is trying to find property that has been fraudulently transferred. We need someone who can go to the courthouse and run property records. It'll involve a lot of investigative and written work, not to mention an inquisitive mind, but it won't require much speaking, except maybe to a few clerks. Think you can handle it?"

"When do I start?" I said. I couldn't wait.

As I left his office, I was especially thankful for God's providence. My experience in the insurance business and in buying an oil company from the profits of my insurance business had taught me how to review company records and titles. I never thought that experience would prove very useful—especially after I became a full-time pastor—but it was custom-made for the type of work W. T. was calling me to do.

I was up the next Monday by about 5 A.M. but made myself stay in bed until about 5:45. Then I made some coffee and got dressed—a suit and tie! on a Monday morning!—and headed out for work.

It was a glorious feeling. Have you ever been really sick and bedridden for a week or more, and then feel good enough just to walk outside and get the mail? The sunlight reintroduces itself, you feel wind brushing against your cheeks, you smell the air, and you think, "Ah, it's good to be alive again"? That's exactly how I felt. I was back in business. For the first time in several months, my spirit was carried by hope.

*I can survive this,* I thought. *As long as I can provide for my family.*

I arrived at the office before W. T. did, and I was shown to my own office, with my own desk. For years, I had taken such items for granted. Of course I had an office. Of course I had a desk. But now, my desk was more beautiful than any desk I had ever seen. And this little office looked more inviting than the Oval Office of the White House.

I wanted to work!

W. T. was a certified peace officer. Technically, I was working as a private investigator—Duane Miller, Private Eye! The real life of a P.I. is nothing like television. It has half the glamour and, thankfully, less than half the danger. For years, I had preached on the value of righteousness. Now, I was delving into the depths of unrighteous acts—and catching people left and right. It's a sobering experience when you realize that your day's labor is liable to cost somebody hundreds of thousands of dollars in fines or even a "vacation" at the federal penitentiary!

One day, during a coffee break—coffee never tastes as good as in the middle of a workday—one of W. T.'s coworkers asked me, "Have you ever thought about seeking your peace officer certification?"

"Not really," I said. "I'm doing fine without it."

"Maybe so, but if you get your certification, you can carry a weapon."

"Then I'm absolutely not interested," I said.

"Why not?"

"If I'm ever in a situation where I need a weapon . . . Well, I don't need to be in that situation!"

I threw myself into work and actually became quite good at it. After all, I didn't have to talk much; I just had to use my brain. On one occasion, while perusing the files of a banker, I found a piece of yellow legal pad paper that read, "One million dollars loaned to . . . " The yellow paper was stuck away in a folder, with no other evidence of the loan anywhere.

It was my job to find out who John Doe was, so I started comparing other records and ran a check on the name. It was fictitious; the person didn't exist. But the money had to go *somewhere*, so I kept looking until I found it—right in the banker's personal account.

Naturally, when I tracked it all down, I was excited. The banker wasn't, however; he's now in jail.

Not long after I went to work for W. T., he sold the agency and moved to another part of the state. I saw my opportunity and jumped at it. I rented an office, hired some people, bought some computers, and suddenly, I was in business. I was able to pick up the contract to work with the same federal agency for whom I had been working before. About half a dozen people from that office would call me virtually on a weekly basis, giving us assignments.

As the S & L crisis heated up and our office kept delivering, we were actually assigned to some top-level cases. My battered and bruised esteem finally began climbing upward. I developed a sense of personal satisfaction and achievement that I hadn't felt in over a year of recovery and unemployment. Being able to support my family allowed me to breathe again. Sometimes, it was even fun.

For a time, it seemed that we had come out on the other side. I still didn't have a voice, but Joylene had a job, we had a house, I had a business, and we attended a church that knew what love is all about. In God's eyes, however, the story was far from over. The testing was really just about to begin.

# chapter six

# Truth
# and
# Consequences

W HEN I WAS IN BIBLE COL-
LEGE, my friends and I were full
of the idealism, enthusiasm, and
the expectancy that comes from preparing for a
life of service to God. We could imagine ourselves
as famous missionaries, stadium evangelists, or
nationally renowned speakers. Though we carried
our share of youthful ambition, for the most part
our hearts were in the right place. One of the
prayers that we prayed, sincerely and frequently, went like this:
"God, I'll go anywhere and do anything."

Many of us learned in the decades that followed that when
we prayed, "God, I'll go anywhere and do anything," we needed
to be willing to go nowhere and to do nothing. It's one thing to
serve God in the bright lights and excitement of being recog-
nized as a "cutting-edge" servant of God. It's another thing altogether to serve Him in a backwater eddy that appears to be
going nowhere.

At times, it may take more faith for us to maintain the right
attitude through an anonymous trial than to preach to fifty
thousand people in a superdome. It may take more faith to
serve faithfully as a youth pastor to three dozen largely unin-

terested kids than to write a book or produce a daily half-hour program.

Most of us didn't want to hear that in Bible college. We wanted to be on the cutting edge. Well, apparently God felt I needed to be sharpened first.

It was great that God had provided me with a job, but in quieter moments, in the deepest parts of my soul, I knew that investigative work was not what God had called me to do. That's important to understand. For a season, I gave myself to a work that I wasn't *called* to do and, to be honest, didn't even particularly *care* to do, but it was what I *could* do. I learned that the will of God for a particular time or season may be nothing more spiritual or elusive than simply whatever we can do. There are times when every Christian will feel like he or she is not on the "cutting edge" of God's plan for his or her life, but remember—Jesus spent 90 percent of His life as a carpenter. Just three short years in active ministry.

As a young man, when I prayed, "Lord, I want to do your will," what I *really* meant was, "Lord, I want to do your will *as long as* it's grandiose, large, and glorious." Sometimes, it will be just that. I still can't believe what God has called me to do today. But at other times we will need to hold on to the verse, "He who is faithful in what is least is faithful also in much."[1]

We must first be faithful in the small things if we expect God to move us into greater things, while at the same time keeping our perspective on just what "great" really means. When our hearts are right, even the seemingly great things we may be doing for God will seem like small things. I've met people who preach to hundreds of thousands of people at a time, yet consider it no different than preaching to five.

Finding God's will is actually not that difficult. God will never ask us to do what we truly don't want to do. What do I mean by that? Eventually, whatever He asks us to do is going to sound good. His call will seize a corner in your heart and you'll want to shout, "Yes! This is going to be okay!"

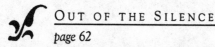

Now, whenever I make that statement, I know that some-body is thinking, "What about Jonah? He didn't want to go to Nineveh. In fact, he ran the other way!"

Remember, Jonah was a prophet. The Bible refers to him as "His servant Jonah. . . the prophet."[2] It's true that Jonah didn't want to go to Nineveh, *but he did want to be a prophet.* Jonah had personal reasons for wanting to avoid Nineveh. He didn't like the particular message God had given him to deliver there, but I believe he always desired to be a prophet, because that's what God created him to be. Sometimes, our overall call-ing may have "seasons of annoyance," but our heart will still be inclined toward God's will.

It's only natural that pastors will occasionally wake up and think, *The last thing I feel like doing today is preaching.* Teachers may say to themselves, "The last person I want to talk to today is anyone under the age of thirty." Employers may mumble, "Please, God, not another personnel dispute." But deep down, in the nether regions of their souls, these people are passion-ately committed to what they are doing.

Now, I believed that God's will was for me to preach. That's what I really wanted to do. I didn't want to be a private inves-tigator. Sure, it was fun sometimes. It provided a paycheck. But it could never excite my soul.

In that case, what did I do? Well, I realized that God's call is always tempered by our ability. For instance, I don't believe God will ever call me to be a professional mechanic. (Who would want to drive a car I worked on, anyway?) My mechani-cal knowledge runs about as deep as putting the car key in the ignition, turning it, and then driving down the road. I can put the automatic transmission into drive, but don't ask me to change a spark plug!

At this point in my life, the desire to preach never left my soul. Even so, preaching was a practical impossibility. I had to let go of it. Right here is where a lot of Christians get stuck in trying to discover God's will for their lives. They cry out on their knees, "Oh God, what do you want me to do?" but never look up to see what opportunities are available. Sometimes, I think God wants to shout at us, "Open your eyes! It's right in front of you! Stop praying and start moving!"

The will of God for our lives consists of doing those things we desire to do, the things we are equipped to do, and the things we have opportunity to do. If something falls into all three of those categories, it is most likely God's call on your life for that time.

So, while my heart was never set on being a private investigator, it *was* set, at that time, on being employed. Past experience had prepared me and given me the ability to do investigative work. And the opportunity to do it was certainly present. So I knew, for that period of my life, that being a private investigator was God's will.

My advice to those who are seeking God's will for their lives is this: Don't stay so busy looking for God's *will* that you miss God. Quit looking for the grandiose and look for the routine. Be satisfied with what God brings your way and then do it with all your heart. God does not dangle opportunity in front of us like a carrot and then have us chase it for the rest of our lives. He wants us to do His will even more than we do! So allow Him to order your steps and trust Him to lead you into His will for your life.

That's what I had to do. And at the same time, the doctors were still trying to figure out what was wrong with me.

## LOOKING FOR ANSWERS

My medical treatment continued unabated. The doctors had ruled out cancer, but there was much yet to do. At one point, I was hooked up to some electrodes and a monitor and given special medication. This entire episode lasted for over four months! My team thought that perhaps I had a rare form of epilepsy and the doctors wanted to check what was going on in my brain. They found . . . nothing.

"Gee, Dad," Lisa teased me, "you should have asked me if there was anything in your head. I could have saved you and

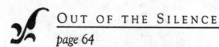

the doctors a whole lot of time and money. We've all known for years that there is nothing up there." Her humor was delightful in spite of the circumstances, particularly since the next few days proved to be some of the darkest in the entire night of my ordeal.

The night began when I asked my doctor if he was testing me for multiple sclerosis (MS). MS is a nervous system disease. I've seen it "up close and personal" a couple of times. I saw the debilitating aspects of the disease during my first stint as a youth pastor, when a woman in the congregation developed MS. I watched a vivacious and fun-loving woman slowly reduced to a bedridden invalid. The oldest and most capable daughter of three became the baby everybody had to care for. Also, to this day, I have a cousin who suffers with the disease. Her courage to continue in spite of her physical limitations is awe-inspiring to me.

I have to confess that even before my lead physician, a neurologist, began testing for the disease, I wondered if MS might be the culprit. Since I had been around people who had the disease, I was somewhat familiar with the symptoms, but I always forced the thought from my mind. I willed myself not to have MS. I'm a struggler. Give me a hill to climb, and I'll climb it. Caleb—one of the two spies who said "Let's go for it! We can take the promised land!"—has always been my role model.

I didn't *want* to have MS, so I was determined to refuse to get it. Or so I thought.

When the doctor began adding two and two and coming up with four, however, denial became an ever-dimming luxury. The medical facts were simply adding up to MS. I was having problems focusing my eyes; that, combined with my voice problem, was apparently indicative of MS, which attacks the nervous system and causes loss of control.

I wasn't about to get it quietly, however. Even when the doctor said, "Yes, Duane, we're checking for MS," I clenched my teeth and inwardly told myself, *It will not be this.*

*Duane Miller*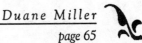

I went through several days of testing for multiple sclerosis, which involved eye exams, CT scans, and a myriad of other things. Finally, on a Friday afternoon the doctor sat me down and said, "Duane, we're 99 percent sure that you have MS."

He might as well have hit me in the forehead with a shovel.

"Come back on Monday," he continued. "By then we'll have the result in from the final test. Then I'll show you how to live with MS."

In stunned disbelief, I arose and shuffled out of his office. I asked myself, *Did I hear him correctly?* I replayed his words in my mind. "Come back on Monday," he had said, *"and I'll show you how to live with MS."* He didn't say, ". . . and we'll talk about how to cure it." He said, ". . . and I'll show you how to live with it."

Yeah, I had heard him correctly. My ability to deny the inevitable was completely blown apart. When a specialist—not just a doctor, mind you, but a *specialist*—tells you that he's 99 percent sure of something, well, how can a rational man argue with that?

The drive home was pure agony. I thought of Joylene and what it would be like for her to see my body slowly devolve into a helpless, nonfunctioning mass of organs, eventually losing its ability to breathe and cutting my life short. MS meant wheelchairs and diapers and the demeaning smell of an invalid who has lost control.

Who has lost control . . . What an irony for a control freak like me. For me, Mr. Control himself, to have a disease that would cause me to lose control, not only of my voice but ultimately my extremities and life systems as well. What the doctor was telling me was that my voice was just my *first* loss. Not only were things not going to get better, *they would grow worse and worse.*

When I came home, Joylene met me at the door. She read my face and adopted its alarm.

"What's wrong, Duane?" she asked. "What did the doctor say?"

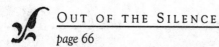

I started to cry. How could I tell the woman who had so faithfully loved me that her trials were really just beginning?

"Come on, Duane," she urged me. "You can tell me."

"He said—" I choked. The words just wouldn't come. I was trained for this, I thought. I had told married men they must leave their girlfriends. I had told parents their kids had just been arrested. I had helped children understand a parent was an alcoholic. I had broken the news of suicide and death to many, many family members. I was used to breaking bad news—that's part of a pastor's job—but these words hurt more than any words I had ever spoken, in part because they were directed to my wife. Each word felt like a buzz saw that chewed up my throat upon its release.

"He said I should come back on Monday and he'd tell me how to live with MS."

Joylene covered her mouth with her hand. She pulled me to her, and her tears began falling on my neck. We held each other and cried. On the one hand, we were relieved finally to have a diagnosis. On the other, we wanted to shout, "Lord, does it have to be *this* disease?"

We stumbled into the living room and sat down, where I began the worst seventy-two hours of my life. As calmly as I could, I explained to Joylene everything I knew about MS. Joylene was silent, as stunned as I had been, while I related the terrible progression and prospect. She has always played the role of an encourager while I have tended to be the realist, so I wanted to give her as real a picture as possible of what the future would be like.

"There's still hope," she insisted. "Didn't the doctor say he was 99 percent sure? That still leaves a chance, doesn't it?"

I looked toward her, but my eyes wouldn't focus. With something—MS, maybe—playing havoc with my body, my eyes couldn't see the woman I had loved all my adult life.

This is what I have to look forward to, I thought.

All I wanted to do was just sit and look at Joylene. Knowing that I would eventually lose my eyesight, I wanted to remem-

*Duane Miller*

ber what she looked like, but my eyes wouldn't cooperate. They wouldn't focus. I wanted to talk to her and tell her how much I loved her, and tell her how much she meant to me, but my voice was so weak, it wouldn't work.

Tears of frustration ran down my cheeks. "Let me see her, God!" I wanted to yell. "Let me talk to her, please, just this once!"

Eventually, my eyes settled down, and I spent the rest of the weekend "storing up" for the future. I didn't watch any television at all. Instead, I sat and stared as Joylene went about her business. I walked around the house, the beautiful house that God had given us, and tried to burn its walls into my memory. I stopped and stared at the photographs and portraits of my daughters.

"Don't forget, brain," I wanted to tell myself. "Whatever you shut down, don't lose your memory of these precious girls."

Where was my faith in this dark hour? I want to be honest with you. As I said, I'm a realist. I don't believe in having a superficial relationship with God. If we're upset with Him, we need to tell Him so, and why. It's okay to get angry with God, as long as we remember that He's still in charge. You see, as hard as it may be for some of you to believe, I never lost my joy, even during this weekend. The reason I never lost it is because *my joy is not dependent upon my happiness.* Job prayed, "Though He slay me, yet will I trust Him,"[3] and that's how I felt. The old Sunday school lessons on the sovereignty of God had stuck. I was angry, sure enough, but I still believed.

Throughout the weekend, when I wasn't staring, Joylene and I prayed, cried, and communicated as best we could. On Sunday, she told me, "I'm going with you tomorrow."

"You don't have to do that," I protested. "You have to work."

"I'll take some time off. I want to talk to the doctor myself."

Joylene saw that I had begun to lose my objectivity. I was so stunned and so beaten down that she felt she couldn't trust my reporting. She wanted to hear what the doctor had to say for herself.

The next morning we entered the doctor's office and were ushered into an examination room. Both of us remained silent. There are few more depressing and sterile places than an examination room when you're about to receive a life-changing prognosis.

My mind swirled with questions about my future. I could almost feel the disease seeping through my body. What would the doctor say? I wondered. How bad was my current condition? How long could I stay out of a wheelchair? When would I finally lose my sight? I wanted answers to all of these questions, and more. If the waiting was finally over, and a diagnosis was finally made, at least I'd get some answers. They weren't the answers I wanted, but they were still answers.

The doctor bounded into the room. He flung open the door and practically shouted, "I've got great news for you, Duane."

I looked up in disbelief.

"I don't understand it. We ran that test fifteen times to be sure, but every time it came back negative. Duane, *you don't have MS.*"

Relief washed over me like a crashing wave. I sighed, dropped my shoulders, and thanked God for the good news. Tears flowed freely and easily, erasing the tension, doubts, and fears that had consumed me all weekend.

As the relief coursed through my soul and I could finally think again, I actually became somewhat angry. The doctor noticed my expression and said, "You don't look too pleased."

"I want to kill you," I responded.

"Why?" he asked, surprised.

"Don't *ever* tell anyone they have an incurable disease until you get all the results in. And for crying out loud, don't ever do it on a Friday afternoon! Do you have any idea what my weekend was like?"

"I'll take it under advisement," he smiled.

*Duane Miller*

We were able to laugh, and I was elated that the diagnosis was not MS, but I prepared myself, once again, for more medical investigation. Given my two major symptoms—throat and vision problems—the doctors were mystified that I didn't have MS. As it turned out, the sight and speech problems were completely unrelated. Apparently I had developed an infection in an optic nerve at that particular time, which eventually cleared up. The timing had thrown the doctors a curveball, and they swung at it.

Thank God it was a strike!

## FALSE HOPE

In June of 1991, I traveled to Philadelphia for some more testing and some intense therapy. After several grueling sessions, my voice came back. It was weak and fragile—not really *my* voice—but at least it was *a* voice. If somebody didn't know me, they would have thought I had a very sore throat or was in the midst of a really bad cold, but they wouldn't have thought I had a permanent disability.

I was as stunned as anyone when I spoke and heard the soft sounds emanate from my throat. One minute I was speaking with a raspy, laryngitis-sounding voice, and the next minute a soft and weak sound was coming out. I still felt the constriction around my throat and I still had to "work" to get the sounds out, but at least the work was producing something.

The doctors were as elated as I was. My birthday passed while I was there so I even made a tape of me singing "Happy Birthday" to myself. By any standard of musical measurement, it was horrible, but it sounded terrific to me. It was a beginning, and I needed some hope.

The doctors encouraged me to call Joylene and talk to her on the phone, but since I was to return to Houston the next day, I decided to wait and tell my sweetheart face to face. I couldn't wait.

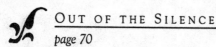

That night, I lay awake thinking, *Well, my throat must be putting itself back together.* I couldn't call myself healed, but this was the first sign of progress in eighteen months.

*A year and a half,* I thought. *That's a long time!* But now my ordeal was drawing to an inexorable end.

There was a new spring in my step as I exited the gateway and saw Joylene and the girls waiting for me at the Houston airport. Joylene smiled—I couldn't wait to see her reaction—and I walked toward her. We hugged, and then I whispered in her ear, "Hi, honey!" It had been eighteen months since she had heard me speak.

Joylene pushed back from me, covered her mouth with her hand, and wept. She threw her arms back around my neck, hugging me and yelling like I had just given her a two-carat diamond ring.

I then spoke to the girls, and they became ecstatic as well. They started jumping up and down. The people standing around us must have thought I had been gone for months.

During the car ride home, the girls' and Joylene's enthusiasm soon led them to begin commiserating with each other about the things they hated and endured during the loss of my voice.

"Oh, the whistle!" Joylene groaned, and the girls laughed.

"Yes!" they shouted in agreement.

"I thought I'd die the next time I heard that whistle," Joylene continued. "I don't care if I never hear another whistle in all my life. I knew you had no other way to get my attention, but I'm so glad you're getting better and you won't have to whistle anymore. I just *hated* being whistled for."

"And now Scott will get to hear how funny you are," Jodi added. Scott was her boyfriend and future husband. He had never heard my real voice.

"I keep telling him how great you are with one-liners, but he's never heard them!"

"It's been a real pain not to be able to talk to you on the phone," Lisa added. "I hated having to talk through Mom."

*Duane Miller*

They admitted that I just hadn't been any fun to be around any more. I couldn't joke, it was difficult to talk, and well, they missed their old dad. Now that the ordeal was over—or so I thought—I laughed along with them.

In the coming days, I was able to speak, but there was still no resonance to my voice. It remained weak and fragile, but you could understand it. We naturally assumed that something had knit back together and I was back on the road to recovery. At times my voice would catch, and I'd lose it again for two or three words, but then it would come right back.

I kept waiting for the full voice to return when, much to my dismay, I lost the soft voice altogether. It was sudden, just a couple of days after it came back, and there was nothing I could do to make it return. I went through the same mechanics, pushing the air up and through my throat, but there was nothing. I gave up trying, but then, about an hour later, my voice came back.

I was terrified. My voice seemed to take on a life of its own. Sometimes it was there, and sometimes it wasn't. I might lose it for one or two words, one or two sentences, and then, even one or two days.

My speech therapist and I worked frantically to bring it back. It was like we were both furiously pulling on a rope to haul my voice over the edge. I was faithful with my exercises, the therapist performed every trick she knew, but the lapses in my voice became greater and greater until, finally, the voice disappeared once again. Within two weeks, I was right back where I had started.

Of course, Joylene and the girls felt terrible for having shared how my loss of voice made life difficult for them. When they tried to apologize, I stopped them. They had hearts of gold. I knew their motives.

If I was angry at all, I was angry at God.

*Lord, you're teasing me,* I thought. I knew it wasn't right to blame God. This wasn't His fault. Even so, getting part of my

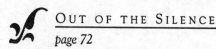

voice back for two weeks felt like having a carrot dangled in front of my face before it was rapidly pulled away.

I went back to the doctors. They couldn't explain why my voice came back and then left. Eventually, they thought that perhaps the nerves had tried to regenerate themselves—which can occasionally happen—but that they just weren't able to do it.

How do you keep loving a God when you know He could so easily have touched you, but chose not to? If my nerves had gotten that close, why couldn't God lift a finger and complete the process? Why, why, why?

## SECOND THOUGHTS

I had as many questions for the doctors as I had for God. Look, I said, if we've ruled out cancer, stress, epilepsy, and MS, then *what is it?*

I was reminded of this period in my life as I watched the 1996 Summer Olympics. There was a young Japanese swimmer whose trademark was a long entry under water. Whereas most of the women surfaced from their dives within fifteen or twenty yards, this young woman stayed under for almost thirty. The consequence was, you could be swimming along in first place, and all the sudden, out of nowhere, this swimmer pops up and you find out you're really in second.

Let me tell you, I could feel for those other swimmers as they waited for the young woman to appear.

Medically, not knowing can be the worst diagnosis you can receive. At least with a diagnosis you know which enemy you're facing, however troublesome. In my circumstance, I had no idea what my body was struggling with.

On a despondent Friday afternoon, my lead physician called me into his office, offered me a chair, then plopped onto his little stool and rolled up right in front of me.

"Duane," he said, "I just want to assure you that I don't think you're crazy."

*Duane Miller*

"Thank you, Doctor," I managed to choke out the words around the tears. "Thank you."

He couldn't offer me relief, but he was offering me understanding. So many times I felt like I was losing my grip on reality. No matter how hard I tried not to dwell on my condition, it was impossible—I felt like I was being choked twenty-four hours a day—and nobody seemed able to figure out why. If nobody could figure out why, nobody could honestly offer me hope for improvement.

The anguish of my physical impairment began to bludgeon my spiritual life, as well. If I hear of anyone who goes through a test as trying as this say he or she never once doubted God, I usually suspect one of two things: that person either is lying or has lost touch with his or her own reality.

The church needs to remember that doubts are a rest stop on the journey of faith, not an assault on it. Some of the most faithful men and women in Scripture wrestled with doubts, even in the midst of their greatest triumphs.

Take Elijah, for instance. In 1 Kings 18, Elijah faced four hundred prophets of Baal in the second most exciting spiritual showdown in history (the first being the crucifixion of Jesus Christ). With what seemed like inspired madness, he and the false prophets engaged in a fantastic duel. Both sides built an altar. The idea was that whoever could call down fire from heaven to consume the altar was the one who was praying to a real God.

The false prophets cut themselves, danced until their feet were raw, and cried out until their throats were sore, but no fire came. Then, in an incredible display of faith and élan, Elijah poured water over his altar, not once, but three times. The altar was so wet that a trough around the base had formed a tiny moat.

Then, with a chutzpah that would be obnoxious in any other situation, Elijah cried out and asked God to consume the altar with fire.

*Poof!*

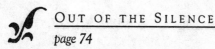

OUT OF THE SILENCE

page 74

Elijah won!

Has such faith ever been equaled? If so, I haven't read or heard about it. Yet just a few days later, where do we see our hero of belief? Lying under a bush, whimpering and complaining about his situation.

Or consider the life of John the Baptist. With the voice of an elephant he boomed out the courageous words of faith to a hungry and sometimes hostile audience. He told Herod what he thought of his marriage to his brother's wife, knowing that he was publicly challenging a man who had the authority to put him to death. When the time came, John willingly gave up his disciples so that they would follow Jesus. God had given him a tremendous reputation and a loyal following, but John was prepared to give it all away.

Don't *ever* underestimate the addiction to power and influence. I've seen pastors hang on to churches for far too long. I've watched the erosion of parachurch ministries as the leader refused to let go long after his time was through. On the other hand, I've seen church members try to reclaim a church from a pastor, and ministry employees try to overthrow a wise and godly leader. Power struggles work both ways. Power is a spiritual drug that turns well-meaning Christians into conniving political partisans once it works its way under their skin. In many ways, power is a form of spiritual heroin.

John, however, was not an addict. Rather than hold on, he chose to give it all up. "Here it is, Jesus," he said by his actions. "My ministry, my disciples, my influence—they're all yours."

What faith! What commitment! What obedience!

Yet after he's arrested and faces his own execution, what does John do? *He has second thoughts!* The man who gave up everything for Jesus begins to wonder if perhaps he wasn't mistaken. He sends his remaining disciples to Jesus so that they can ask Him, "Are you really the one we should be looking for, or will another come after you?"[4]

What happened in the lives of these two men? John and Elijah proved that faith "leaks!" Doubts are a bump in the road of every Christian's life. Instead of denying them, we need to admit them and then confront them.

That's what I had to do. I would love to tell you that throughout these difficult years I stood my ground as a mighty man of faith. I would love to tell you that I never doubted that God would heal me. I would love to tell you that I just knew that my life and ministry would be restored.

The only problem is, if I told you those things, I would be lying. There were days when I cried out to the Lord, "What are you doing, God? Why don't You help me?" I sounded like the psalmist Asaph crying out, "Will the Lord cast off forever? / And will He be favorable no more? / Has His mercy ceased forever? / Has His promise failed forevermore? / Has God forgotten to be gracious? / Has He in anger shut up His tender mercies?"[5]

I didn't even want to go to church anymore. I couldn't sing, so worship was more frustrating than joyful. I listened to a great sermon, which, more than anything else, reminded me of my own inability to preach. It was hard feeling sorry for someone who asked for prayer for a broken toe.

Instead of being an encouragement to my faith, attending church became an assault on my faith—and I had nowhere else to turn.

I was desperate. I wondered if I'd been totally forgotten and abandoned. And even looking back, I believe that to deny those feelings rather than express them would be a very big mistake. Denial is not a demonstration of great faith; it's simply Pollyanna's approach to bad news. Jesus said, "I am the way, the *truth*, and the life."[6] As His disciples, we, too, should embrace truth—even the truth of our doubts.

Here was the real danger of my situation: The enemy was trying to turn my illness into a stronghold. His first plan was to alienate me from the body of Christ.

To survive, I'd have to discover an entirely new strength, because I was playing by a completely new set of rules.

# It's
# Miller
# Time!

HAVE YOU EVER FELT VERY, VERY lonely, wishing more than anything else that a particular friend would call—and then they do?

That's what happened to me in the fall of 1991. We had been in Houston for about nine months. I was settled into my job, the doctors were still struggling to develop a diagnosis, and life kept marching forward.

Living without teaching, however, felt like living without a right arm. You keep trying to reach out for something, and then you realize the arm isn't there. I'd think of a good sermon illustration, I'd be moved by a particular passage, I'd get that burning feeling in my soul, and then I'd remember, "Oh yeah—I can't preach."

Just when I was particularly missing my friend, the pulpit, I got a call from Cherie Young. The Catacombs class wanted me to speak at their fall retreat. I was both confounded and delighted. This was an incredible act of faith on their part. My voice had its good days and its bad days, but even the good days were iffy. Predicting what my voice would be like a month ahead of time was like predicting July's weather in May.

"I'm not sure, Cherie," I protested.

"About what?" she asked.

"First, that you'll be able to understand me; and second, that my voice will even last."

I had learned to make myself heard by using guttural pressure, forcing up the air, and screaming at the top of my lungs. The result still sounded incredibly hoarse, but if I was one-on-one with someone, he or she could understand 80 to 90 percent of what I was saying. Translating that into a group setting seemed daunting.

"It'll work out," she insisted.

"You need to have a plan B," I warned.

"We will," she assured me.

Preparing for the retreat did wonders for my soul. Studying and teaching God's Word is what God created me to do, and while preparing for the retreat I felt like a formerly hooked fish who had been let loose in the water once again.

The weekend of the retreat arrived. Even though everybody in the room had heard me speak for hours upon hours, I was as preoccupied before the first session as a recent seminary graduate is before his first sermon. I felt positive about the content of my talk but anxious about my voice and my ability to be heard. When I had practiced trying to speak up at home, I met with less than stellar results. I knew it would take a miracle for this retreat to come off, and to be honest with you, I was ready for a miracle!

We went through the singing, the get-acquainted games, and the other retreat staples, and soon it was time for me to stand up and speak. As soon as I stood up front, I was caught short when I noticed that everybody was wearing a jacket. I had been so focused on getting ready for my talk that the observation hadn't registered.

*Hmmm,* I thought. *It doesn't seem cold in here . . .*

And then, before I could get into my teaching, all of them stood up, took off their jackets, and turned around. Each had a message stenciled on the back of a T-shirt that read: "It's Miller Time!"

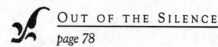

Tears stung my eyes and salted my mouth, putting me at ease. I knew I was home. However the teaching went, love had already secured the evening.

I wish I could tell you that a miracle was performed that night, that somehow, God gave me the strength to preach a normal session. He didn't. I was trying so hard to raise my voice that I kept choking, and then my throat went into spasms. I was able to speak for about ten minutes, and then I was done. Cherie made an announcement, asking the class members to let me be quiet when I wasn't speaking so that my throat could rest, but the next day, I was still able to go just ten or fifteen minutes during each of the three sessions.

It was a bitter experience. I had gotten a "taste" of teaching again, but I was also forced to admit how incapable of teaching I really was. If the realization was going to happen anywhere, however, I was thankful it happened here, where I could be surrounded by such loving people. One of the things I love about the Catacombs class is that they're real. Instead of just saying, "That's okay," people started crying. They missed hearing me and I missed speaking to them. We didn't have to mask our disappointment with pious platitudes:

"That's all right, Duane, God still really blessed me."

"Probably for the best that it worked out like it did—gave us more time to sing and worship."

Instead, they could say to me, "I'm sorry, Duane, I really wanted to hear all that you had to say." And I could respond, "And I'm sorry—I really wanted to speak longer." By the end of the weekend we simply sat around and shared our sorrow, not afraid to ask the question, "Why, Lord, why?"

Well, we were about to find out.

## DIAGNOSIS

"Spasmodic dysphonia."

"Spasma—say what?"

"Spasmodic dysphonia. That's our diagnosis."

*Duane Miller*

After over eighteen months of testing, prodding, poking, and sticking, the doctors had a diagnosis.

"What's that?" I asked.

The doctor smiled. "In layman's terms, it's the label we use when we can't define a voice malady in any other way."

I felt Joylene's fingers press into my arm as the doctor told us how rare my case was. You see, spasmodic dysphonia itself is very rare—say, one in a million people get it. But my version was even more rare than that. In most cases of spasmodic dysphonia, one or both of the vocal cords become paralyzed. This can be treated by an injection in the throat, which causes the muscles to relax and the speech to return. Patients can speak for about four to five months, at which time they must receive another injection.

In my case, however, neither of my vocal cords was paralyzed—they were just limp. In other words, I was one in a million out of that first one in a million! An injection to relax my throat muscles would have made my situation *worse*. Because my circumstances were so rare, doctors had no other treatment on the books.

Now, here's where the situation gets exciting. Because my case was so rare, I became an object of discussion for virtually every doctor around the world who had any recognizable credentials in the area of neuro-speech motor skills. At least sixty-three doctors have personally examined me, including physicians who have treated such world-renowned singers as Luciano Pavarotti, Frank Sinatra, Larry Gatlin, and Bruce Springsteen (who just about run the gamut of music!).

Do you realize what God was doing? Before He stepped in, He wanted it to be known that even the best and brightest in the world wouldn't be able to enact a cure. Not a single expert would be able to say he or she could have helped me. It was as if God was saying, "All right, experts, take your best shots."

The glory would be all His.

He also, apparently, wanted documentation. Part of my extensive examination process involved making and keeping videotapes of my throat. Just about every doctor who examined me would put a flexible scope down my throat and videotape the examination. No one would ever be able to question whether my situation was serious.

Here's what the doctors discovered.

If you were to look down your own throat, you would see that it comes to a "V" at the bottom. You would notice that the surfaces of what you see are slick-smooth in their appearance and that there is a small "bump" on each side of your throat, very near the bottom. Those bumps are small pieces of fat called false cords. When you get laryngitis and your throat is swollen, the false cords come together above your real vocal cords and create a raspy sound.

The false cords are not designed to sustain speech over a long period of time, but since my real cords did not move, they were all I had to make sound. Constant use, however, caused them to become abraded. Ultimately, scar tissue formed in the abrasions, and the result looked like the knees of a kid who had fallen on concrete, scraping the skin off his knee cap and forming bumpy scabs. What had been slick-smooth in its appearance became rough and gnarly.

This entire process was faithfully recorded during each examination. The change is observable, like time-lapse photography, when you put the tapes together.

One of my doctors arrived at a symposium in Switzerland where an internationally renowned group of throat doctors gathered. You know what I'm talking about—it's one of those conferences where the best of the best come together to get even better.

My doctor decided to take a videotape of my throat to the symposium, hoping to get some additional opinions and to see if any of these world-renowned doctors had any new ideas to offer for treatment. He might as well have taken a box of suckers to a day care. When a few doctors saw the limp condition of my vocal cords and the incredible amount of scar tissue that had formed on my false cords, they were so enthralled that they

*Duane Miller*

took the video downstairs, put it up on the big screen, and showed it to all the physicians in the main room.

I was a bigger hit than Arnold Schwarzenegger. Okay, so not a single doctor would have been able to identify me if I had walked into the room, but they sure knew what my throat looked like!

Interest over my video erased most of the agenda, and for several days, the world's best throat specialists discussed my condition. This is the part that's so exciting. The best of the best looked at my situation not only individually but also collectively, and together they arrived at the same conclusion: The virus I'd had in January of 1990 had invaded my vocal cords and destroyed the nerves.

My physician shared all this with me and Joylene when he got back. At first, I was encouraged. Imagine all those world-famous specialists discussing my case! I couldn't ask for more. Surely one of them would have some new treatment or suggestion.

"So what does all this mean?" I asked. "What's the final prognosis for recovery?"

"Zero," the doctor said, shaking his head. I felt like a bullet shot through my throat. The best doctors in the world had talked about my situation for several days and came up with *nothing*?

"I'm sorry," the doctor explained. "If the nerves were going to regenerate, they would have done so long ago. It is simply not going to happen."

The doctor paused. He knew how much the next words were going to hurt, but he had to say them anyway. "For all practical purposes, you should now consider yourself permanently disabled."

*Permanently disabled!* I almost couldn't catch my breath.

Finally, trying to inject some hope into the situation, I said, "Well, at least I can squeak."

"Well," the doctor answered, and from his tone I knew that the worst was yet to come, "I'm sorry to tell you this, but it was the opinion of all the doctors there that you will eventually wear away the surfaces of the false cords to the point that they can no longer 'get together.' What little ability you have to speak now, using your scarred false cords, will disappear entirely."

In case I didn't understand the implications, he added, "You will become completely mute."

I could think of only one question. "How long?"

"It's hard to say," he answered. "Probably late '94 or early '95 at the latest. By then you won't be able to make a sound."

I sat there in stunned silence. There was no positive face to paint on this picture. The fact that my doctor was speaking the collective opinion of the world's best specialists meant that there was really no point in getting a second opinion. I had been given a fifth, sixth, and hundredth opinion, and all of them agreed: I was going to lose my voice completely. Within three years, I'd be completely mute. This preacher had preached his last sermon.

Joylene just broke inside. She had coped with my disability by looking forward to the day when my voice would return. When she realized that it wouldn't, that in fact I'd one day be completely mute, she just fell apart inside. I watched as she pulled her hand from around my arm and covered her eyes. Soon, her back was heaving deep sobs of pain, releasing months and months of pent-up frustration and weariness. I reached over and rubbed her on the back. I had been married to this woman for over twenty years, and I never remembered seeing her cry so hard.

This might sound odd, but there was no better gift she could have given to me at that moment. As I whispered words of encouragement and attempted to caress my wife back into calm, my own heart stayed amazingly at ease. By focusing on someone else's pain, my own pain seemed less severe.

On our way home, we stopped by the Singletons. David is a fellow singer, an elder at Memorial Drive Presbyterian Church, and a former business associate; and he and his sweet wife, Maureen, are some of our dearest friends. I'm not sure exactly why we stopped. Maybe we just needed to see a friendly face. Maybe we needed to talk about something else, reminisce, share old "war stories." Whatever the reason, the Singletons were paid a visit.

After our time together, David walked us out to our car. As I sat behind the steering wheel and reached for the ignition, David leaned against the car and spoke through the window I had rolled down.

"So what's up, Duane?" he asked. "What are the doctors saying, really, about your recovery?"

I didn't want to be a burden on my friends. I didn't want them to have to suffer as we were suffering, but David's tone was so genuine that I knew he deserved to know the truth. I swallowed (painfully) hard and said, "They told me I'll never get better, that in fact I'll get worse." I paused, trying to keep my composure. "They said within another two years, I'll lose my voice completely."

David's eyes rimmed with tears and his lip started quivering as he leaned through the car window to hug me. Sobbing, he leaned back, grabbed my throat, and said, "This can't be. God won't let it happen."

I put my hand over his. I was thankful for his compassion but skeptical of his analysis. God had *already* let it happen. What was to keep Him from taking it a step further?

## LEARNING TO COPE

We wanted to be as honest as possible with our daughters, so I called them up to tell them. I don't know if it was because of my sadness or what, but my voice seemed even worse than usual. It had more hoarseness to it, so when I struggled to bring out the sound, it truly sounded garbled. But I was determined to make this call while I still had half a voice left. This time, I insisted that I, not Joylene, place the call.

"I'm sorry," the young woman on the other end of the line said. "What did you want?"

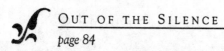

"I'd like to speak to Jodi, please." I winced at the way my voice came out.

The young woman turned from the phone and said, "I think we got another crank caller. This guy's trying to sound sexy or something."

"What's he saying?" someone asked.

"I'm not sure, I can't understand him."

"Wait—that might be my father." I heard Jodi's voice in the background, and my heart just ached. I always wanted my daughters to be proud of their father. Sure, every daughter goes through the stage where she's a bit embarrassed by her father's clothing, his "old fashioned" speech, and the other generally unforgivable sins of being over forty years old. But eventually, daughters grow out of it, and I wanted mine to be proud of the man who loved them more than they could ever possibly know.

To think that Jodi had to cope with roommates who thought her father sounded like an obscene caller . . .

That was a rough phone call. I didn't want to let it happen again, so Joylene went back to making most of my calls for me.

*I can fight this thing*, I thought, *but I can't beat it*. It was a tremendously difficult realization to make.

Life changed from that day forward. Some changes were subtle, others monumental. The most significant change was the growing recognition that church was no longer my favorite place to be. For years, Sunday morning had been the highlight of my week. I loved to sing and I loved to teach and I loved to fellowship with God's people. Now, I couldn't do any of that. Sure, I could show up, but I couldn't sing during worship. I couldn't teach. And it was difficult to fellowship when people had to keep leaning forward and ask me, "What? I'm sorry, I didn't get that last comment."

On Christmas Eve, I sat in the service, stunned, weary, and broken. Christmas Eve services are 80 percent hymn-singing at most churches, and ours is no exception. That made this service even more difficult than usual for me. After about fifteen minutes, I noticed that something else seemed wrong, but I couldn't quite put my finger on it. Finally, I looked to my right, and it hit me. Joylene had stopped singing too.

"Joylene," I whispered, "you don't have to stop singing just because I can't sing."

Joylene looked at me with a painful smile, then shook her head "No." She wouldn't sing if I couldn't. She knew what singing meant to me, and she just literally could not do it.

"Please?" I said.

Again, Joylene shook her head "No." She was adamant. If my singing days were done, hers were as well.

We stood together in the midst of what should be a Christian's biggest celebration of the year, our spirits anchored to the ground.

## A DISABLED DAD

It might seem like a small and subtle distinction, but to our family, the realization that I was no longer "sick" but "permanently disabled" made a big difference. I'll always be thankful, however, for the way our daughters coped.

One of the most difficult aspects of my malady for me was knowing that my daughters had to work to help pay for their college expenses. I would have loved to have enabled them to devote full-time to their studies and the educational and social environment of a college campus. Our reduced income and my added therapy expenses, however, just wouldn't stretch that far. One time, I had suggested that perhaps I could put some of my therapy off until after the girls were out of college, but they wouldn't hear of it.

"No, Daddy, I'm fine, really. I even *like* my job. I'd do it for free!" (Not even a daddy is that naive!)

But perhaps the most difficult times of all came when my daughters were actually home. These were the girls I had once bathed, diapered, and fed. I had carried them when their little legs got too tired, I had sung them to sleep at night, and I had protected them when they were frightened by a dog or a thunderstorm.

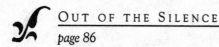

Now, the roles reversed. Almost intuitively, they learned how to cope with a disabled father. They soon learned to initiate conversation with friends or strangers to spare me the pain or embarrassment of attempting a feeble answer. They developed the art of slipping in front of me at the grocery store line so they could answer when the cashier asked, "Paper or plastic?" Sounding casual, they asked to drive when they knew we'd be going to a bank or fast food restaurant. Because they loved me, these interferences were never overt. They didn't say, "Daddy, since you can't talk, let me drive to the bank."

But they knew what was going on, and I knew what was going on. The caregiver had become the carereceiver.

Both of my girls passed up excellent opportunities to study and travel overseas. As this book was being written, I found out that Lisa even took a course in sign language to prepare herself for the time when that would be my primary mode of communication.

I was touched, humbled, and moved beyond measure.

Jodi and Lisa were both Zetas. The sorority sisters met for prayer on a weekly basis, and every week, my name was put on the top of the prayer list. Jodi and Lisa were frequently asked for updates on my progress, and the Zetas dutifully followed every victory and setback in my struggle.

Eventually, they asked Jodi if I'd come and lead a Bible study for them. They had heard so much about me and had prayed for me for so long that they wanted to meet me. Jodi called me with the invitation and I smiled. How could I refuse? Realizing that these women, most of whom had never met me, were praying for me on a weekly basis, I felt like I had no choice. In fact, I was thrilled to do it (perhaps even a little *too* thrilled from Joylene's point of view!).

"This is great," I croaked out when I stood in front of my daughter's sorority sisters. They were a beautiful, intelligent bunch, exactly the crowd I'd want my daughters to claim as their friends. "I'm honored to be here. I spent half my energies in college trying to be in this position, having the rapt attention of 250 sorority women. If I'd known losing my voice was the ticket it took, I would've done this twenty years ago!"

## BACK IN THE SADDLE

Early in 1992, the teacher in our Catacombs class needed to step down from his role for personal reasons, and God impressed on Cherie Young that I was to resume my former duties as teacher of the class. The only problem was, Cherie was the *only* one God spoke to, and few believed her—including me.

Without telling me, Cherie went to the minister of education and said, "I think Duane should teach the Catacombs class."

"You think *what?*"

Not surprisingly, he was a bit skeptical—as I would be, were I in his place. I've led a church, so I know the responsibilities, and I can completely understand if that pastor thought Cherie had begun to lose her mind. The Catacombs class was the most successful Sunday school class in a very large church; it wasn't something to play around with. And why would people listen to a guy with a scratchy, raspy, hard-to-understand voice?

Cherie wouldn't let up. At one point her husband said, "Cherie, don't you think it's time to let it go?"

Cherie shot back, "I won't let go. You can either fight this battle with me, or I'll do it on my own."

When she encountered ongoing resistance, she went to the very top—Dr. John Bisagno himself.

Dr. John Bisagno, senior pastor of Houston's First Baptist Church, is a tremendous man of God. He has a huge, caring heart. Brother John listened to Cherie and finally said, "Let's try it over the summer."

Brother John's wisdom was evident. During the summer, families are on vacation, fewer people are visiting, and it would be the perfect time to prove to Cherie that this crazy idea of hers just wouldn't work.

I had no idea how much legwork had gone on when Cherie approached me in the spring of 1992 and asked me to consider teaching the Catacombs class once again. I was so touched I felt my knees buckle. At first, I couldn't believe the class would want to give me another chance after the disastrous retreat, but I was deeply moved by their willingness to give it a try. Since the retreat, I had begun working with a therapist and had learned what caused the choking when I raised my voice to speak to a crowd. I spent several weeks teaching myself how to breathe, and I thought, maybe, just maybe, this might actually work.

Still, I wanted to be sure that Cherie knew what she was doing. "Are you absolutely sure that this is what you want to do?" I asked her.

"Absolutely."

"But why would people want to listen to this?" I pointed to my throat.

"If you'll teach, we'll listen," Cherie said. Her tone reminded me of my dad's. I knew not to argue.

One "minor" problem we encountered was procuring a microphone sensitive enough to pick up my weak voice and directional enough to shut out ambient room noise. A friend of mine who is a sound engineer rigged up a microphone—the same kind that many professional singers wear in concerts—that, when pressed directly against my lips, was able to take what little voice I had and broadcast it to the class.

It was exhilarating for me during a timespan in my life when every door was closing to have such a precious door fly wide open. I realized that I might have very little time left and I needed to use the few remaining months wisely. After that, I'd never be able to teach again. If these people were willing to decipher my poor excuse for a voice, I was willing to throw it at them for as long as I could.

I accepted Cherie's offer, never dreaming that God was setting me up for the life changing event that would eventually take place right there in that Sunday school class on January 17, 1993.

# chapter eight

# My Great-Great-Great-Great-Great-Great-Grandfather Job

J UST WHEN I STARTED TEACH-
ING THE class again, financial disaster
approached us like a swirling tornado. It
began in May of 1992. For over a year, work had
continued to pour in from the federal agency. We
received several faxes a day, and often several
new assignments a week. All reports were that
the agency was more than satisfied with our work.

But in May, the contracts abruptly stopped
coming. Since I had been working for about a dozen different
individuals within the agency, it seemed rather odd that the
work would stop all at once—unless there was some directive
from on high.

At first, I didn't let it bother me. We were still working on
several assignments and there are lulls in just about every business. As the man responsible to pay the bills, however, I began
to be anxious as each case was completed and no new cases
came forward to pick up the slack.

The inevitable eventually happened. We completed the last
assignment and then had absolutely nothing to do. There were
no words of reprimand from the agency, nothing to signify that
our work had been less than satisfactory, so I decided to pay a

visit to the agency. I talked with my primary contact and tried to keep the conversation as good-natured as possible.

"Hey, what's up?" I said. "I haven't heard from you guys in ten days. My fax machine is getting cobwebs in it."

He laughed, and I laughed with him.

"Did I make somebody angry?" I asked. "Did I do something wrong?"

"Absolutely not," the man replied. "We're just doing a little reorganization over here. You'll hear from us soon enough."

I knew that the first part was true—they really were undergoing major reorganization—so I just assumed that the second part must be true as well.

"All right," I said, "I'll be here when you need me."

I stood up, and we shook hands. He was smiling, even though he knew that I'd never work with him again.

I didn't know that, however, and I left his office in a relatively upbeat mood. *It'll come back*, I thought. *I just have to wait this out for another couple weeks.*

A month passed, and still my fax machine lay idle. My overhead didn't go down a penny, but my revenue plummeted to zero. That's what was so difficult to take. We're not talking about beach erosion, here. We're talking about an economic tsunami: one minute, there was a beach; the next minute, there was only water.

It was time to think about other options. I went home and opened the mail—it was about the only thing to do—and noticed a letter from our group insurance carrier. Normally, I liked getting these letters. Half the time, they had checks in them. We could certainly use a check, however small, so I eagerly tore open the envelope.

"Hmmm, no check," I muttered to myself, then just about dropped to the floor when I saw bills totaling $22,000 fall out.

"WHAT'S THIS?"

I quickly scanned the cover letter, not wanting to believe that what I was reading was really true.

 OUT OF THE SILENCE

"Dear Mr. Miller," the letter began. "After contacting your physician, we have learned that your condition has been downgraded to that of a permanent disability. You are hereby notified that any further treatment will be considered experimental and is therefore not covered under your policy. Furthermore, we have determined that the enclosed bills represent experimental treatment and therefore are also not covered under your existing policy. Even though they were preapproved, you will be solely responsible for their payment."

"Now you tell me!" I wanted to shout. Why didn't they let me know before I underwent the treatment? I dropped onto the stool in our kitchen, rubbing my forehead with my hand. That meant no more speech therapy. It also meant trying to find a way to pay over $20,000 worth of bills that we had no idea we'd be held responsible for.

At that moment, with my primary income having dropped to zero, $22,000 felt like a close cousin to the national debt. *There has to be some way out of this,* I thought. When I reviewed our options, however, I couldn't find one. We had no savings with which to fight this decision in the judicial courts. We were stuck.

Our kids were in school and working, we were struggling just to pay our bills, and now our total indebtedness had climbed to astronomical proportions just as my income crashed to next to nothing.

I felt like I had stepped inside the ring with Muhammad Ali in his prime and was reeling from a one-two punch that sent me sprawling onto the canvas.

The next month, July of 1992, I received yet another letter. This one was from the insurance company that was paying my disability checks. "Dear Mr. Miller," the letter began, "After reevaluating your condition, we have determined that it does not fall under the definition that the Social Security Administration gives to disability. Therefore, your condition no longer qualifies as a disability under the terms of your policy, and we are suspending the payments which you have heretofore received."

*Great*, I thought, *just great*. One insurance company stops paying me because I'm permanently disabled; the other stops paying me because I'm not really disabled.

I wanted to call my mom and tell her I was sure we had Jewish blood somewhere.

"What makes you think that?" she'd ask.

"Because I *must* be related to Job."

My income had now gone from thousands to hundreds to nothing. My hope didn't wilt like a plant in a drought; it exploded like a potato in a microwave. I felt helpless, especially knowing that my condition was going to get worse. The doctor had been very clear that I had no hope of improvement.

In the span of three months, I lost my job, lost any hope of further treatment on my throat, picked up $22,000 in medical bills, and then lost the only remaining income I had been providing to my family through the disability policy.

"All right, God" I prayed. "Are you done playing with me, yet? How much more do you think I can take? I'm only human, remember?"

After I worked off my steam in prayer, I told the news to Joylene. She had gotten so used to receiving bad news that this last hit from the disability insurance carrier was practically expected. We found it was easier to cope by not talking about it. When we tried to discuss our options, the futility of our situation would blow its bad breath back into our faces and cause nothing but further tension and uneasiness. To make matters worse, the increased stress made my throat go into spasms even more frequently.

Sleep became a stubborn stranger. I spent many nights sitting up in the living room, worrying and waiting for morning to bring another frustrating day.

I want to be as honest as possible here. If at that time I didn't have a ministry outlet, I very well may have gone into a free fall

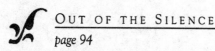

of despair. My attitude had grown so bad that I would have had to improve it just to join Elijah under the juniper tree!

## PRACTICAL CHRISTIANITY

Like Elijah, I had seen and experienced the blessings of God many times throughout my life. But just as it was perceived by Elijah, all of those experiences seemed buried in the past by the bleak and frightening future. It was inevitable that I would ask, "Is it really worth it to carry on?"

And like Job, I had well-meaning people inadvertently pour salt into my wounds with statements like, "Why don't you just let it go, Duane? Just forget about your problems; God will take care of them."

I'd smile, but inwardly I'd think, *How do I do that? How do I just "forget" something that literally has me by the throat and seems to be squeezing the very life out of me?*

I know preachers are supposed to have all the answers, to be "together" and "spiritual" at all times (what does that mean, anyway?). Let me tell you something that was forged in the fiery pit of my darkest trial: When I minister to people today, I am very slow to offer empty platitudes. I swallow my words three or four times before I'll risk saying anything that sounds like a quick and easy recipe for peace.

Instead of using platitudes, I've learned the power of silence and touch. I put my arms around them, I cry with them, I pray with them, I empathize with their pain and even help them to express the unmentionable: fear. *Of course you're scared,* I'll tell them. *I would be too.*

Time after time, I've seen clouds leave their faces when a pastor gives them permission to be afraid. I've learned this the hard way. It took three torturous years, but I think just about every self-righteous and judgmental bone in my body has been broken at least two or three times!

The only faith I had at this point was not faith that I would be healed, or that I would suddenly find a great job, or even that a check would fall out of heaven. Instead, ironically enough, it was faith that God had called me to teach. Preparing for and addressing the Catacombs class each Sunday helped to keep me sane. In the midst of bad report after bad report, and financial blow after financial blow, at least I could lose myself in God's Word and in explaining Scripture to others.

Apparently, the class was also a blessing to the members. In spite of the fears that my voice problem would dampen attendance, the number of people coming every Sunday actually increased. That this happened over the traditionally slow summer months made it all the more remarkable.

Yet the price I had to pay for teaching the class climbed with every passing week. When I spoke for one hour on Sunday, I lit a painful fire in the back of my throat that didn't go out until late Tuesday or early Wednesday. Unfortunately, the doctor's prediction that my situation would eventually grow worse was coming true.

I'm not stupid. I knew what was coming, and it seemed that if I couldn't communicate God's Word orally, I'd have to do it some other way.

## SOUL THERAPY

The desire to write had been latent within me for some time. My responsibilities as associate and senior pastor had led me to write a number of curricula, letters, columns, and the like, and I have always received great feedback from these projects.

"You ought to write more, Pastor," had been a frequent comment given to me on Sunday mornings.

"I'll write more when God creates an eighth day," I had shot back. There was just never enough time to put other projects down and pick up the pen (or, in today's world, switch on the computer).

Well, now I had the time, so I decided that maybe God's will for my life was taking another direction. I decided to write a newsletter. Over the years, I had subscribed to a number of newsletters myself, covering everything from business to poli-

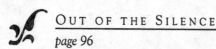

tics to Christian living. The ones I enjoyed the most were the ones that gave a personal perspective on universal issues. I wanted to write helpful information on the Christian life—something that Christians could use to grow in their faith.

What to call it? I remembered a gift I had been given several years prior by the members of one of my Sunday school classes—a beautiful black leather Bible. Inside the front cover each member had inscribed an encouragement along with his or her signature. One of the members wrote, "Duane, thank you for making Christianity practical for me." That comment touched me more than any of the others, because that was exactly my aim. If we couldn't use our faith Monday through Saturday, I didn't see much point in coming to church on Sunday. Our God and His gospel are very pragmatic.

With this newsletter, the last thing I wanted to do was get sidetracked in debating the finer points of theology. As far as I'm concerned, it doesn't really matter much if a man living in sin is backslidden (Arminian theology) or never really saved (Calvinist). The point is, he's lost and needs Jesus (practical Christianity). Instead of sitting around and trying to describe what kind of fire is enveloping our fellow man, we need to pick up the "extinguisher" of God's truth and put him out!

The thought of writing a book seemed too daunting, but a newsletter sounded much more "doable." I approached a friend of mine who was an attorney and ran the idea by him.

"That's not a bad idea, Duane," he said, "but I'd encourage you to keep your day job until this takes off." (He didn't know my "day job" had already collapsed.)

"Why don't we set up a nonprofit organization?" he continued. "That way, if someone wants to contribute twenty dollars for stamps, they can legally deduct it."

The next morning, I realized that if I was going to receive any donations at all, I needed a board to keep me accountable for those gifts. I spent the next several days praying and thinking about men to serve on my board.

Though my speech therapy had stopped because of lack of insurance coverage, I sometimes look back and see that God had something else—soul therapy—in mind. Nothing removes a person's anxieties like getting involved in doing something for the kingdom of God. Finally, my energies were being used to serve God instead of feeling sorry for myself. I didn't expect *Practical Christianity* to become a huge ministry, but it was helpful to have my mind preoccupied with positive initiatives and plans rather than being polluted by frustrating and sometimes infuriating news.

To all those who are weighed down by the burden of life, I encourage you, find *something* to do to serve God. When the great missionary, Hudson Taylor, was completely bedridden, he had someone tape a map to the wall so he could intercede for God's work. He couldn't preach a sermon, he couldn't pass out food, he couldn't even lift a pencil to write an encouraging letter, but he could pray.

We need that same attitude.

For the moment, I was alive again. I settled on seven men and invited them to our house for an organizational meeting. Now things were moving along.

"This is great, Duane," one of them said, "and I appreciate the opportunity to meet all these godly men. But why are we here?"

I shared my vision about the newsletter and how I needed a board of directors to help guide the small ministry and any of the donations that might be received. Every individual agreed to serve, and *Practical Christianity* was born.

The next morning, instead of sitting around and staring at the walls, I sat down in front of a computer and began writing the first issue. The ideas came freely and easily, and the first issue fell together almost by itself.

Of course, a newsletter has to go to somebody, so I rifled through my Rolodex and sent an issue to anyone who had ever had sufficiently poor foresight to provide me with his or her business card. If I had their address, they got a newsletter.

Along with the first issue, I sent an introductory letter that basically said, "Hi! This is what I'm doing for ministry now. If the doctors are right, it may be the only ministry I have left. If you don't want to be on my mailing list, please let me know and I'll drop your name. Otherwise you will receive a new issue of *Practical Christianity* every three weeks. If you want to help me with the postage, great. If not, just read it and enjoy it."

The first issue was mailed out the day before Thanksgiving in 1992. I sent out about four hundred copies, and just two people wrote back to request being dropped from my mailing list. That was definitely encouraging.

The financial blows we had endured a few months earlier still stung, but with the advent of this writing career, I had hope again. In fact, I felt that maybe I really could write a book after all. In December, I got serious and put together a proposal. I outlined a book, wrote a sample chapter, fleshed out a couple of others, and sent the entire package to two Christian publishers with whom I had personal contact.

Sending the packages out provided a great measure of hope, and my soul needed hope as much as a suffocating man needs oxygen.

## FAMILY MATTERS

A couple of weeks before Christmas, Jodi and Scott called Joylene, their voices dripping with enthusiasm. "We found this small microphone," they said. "You carry the box in your pocket, and it allows people to hear you. We want to buy it for Dad for Christmas."

Though my writing endeavors had given me a lighter heart, the increased pain in my throat created a tender spot in my soul. Joylene thought it might be best not to remind me of this on Christmas morning.

"I'm sorry, Jodi," Joylene said. "It's a great idea and I know you mean well, but this just isn't the time. Maybe in six months, but right now, I'm afraid your father wouldn't take it very well."

She was right.

But Jodi never stopped believing. One night, over the Christmas holidays, she slipped into our room as Joylene and I were watching television in bed. Jodi climbed in between us, the way she'd done when she was a little girl, and just lay there, silent, for quite awhile. Finally, she spoke.

"Dad," she said, "I really feel that you're going to be healed."

Her voice carried such an astonishing assurance that I didn't have the heart to disagree with her. "Thanks, Peanut," I said, giving her shoulders a squeeze. I felt grateful for her intentions, but inside, I almost felt sorry for her. She just didn't realize what was up ahead, and I didn't want her to be disappointed.

Jodi wasn't alone in her optimism. Joylene's father was adamant in his insistence that my malady was a temporary situation that God would eventually heal.

"Duane," he said, with the confidence of an evangelist pointing out the Scriptures, "God has given me Ezekiel 3:26-27. He's told me that Ezekiel's story will be your story."

I vaguely remembered the passage, but just to be sure, he read it out loud, his voice full of confidence in its truth:

*"I will make your tongue cling to the roof of your mouth, so that you shall be mute and not be one to rebuke them, for they are a rebellious house. But when I speak with you, I will open your mouth, and you shall say to them, 'Thus says the Lord GOD.' He who hears, let him hear; and he who refuses, let him refuse; for they are a rebellious house."*

"Ezekiel's mute condition wasn't permanent," Joylene's dad assured me. "Look at 33:21-22."

*And it came to pass in the twelfth year of our captivity, in the tenth month, on the fifth day of the month, that one who had escaped from Jerusalem came to me and said, "The city has been captured!" Now the hand of the LORD had been upon me the evening before the man came who had escaped. And He had*

*opened my mouth; so when he came to me in the morning, my mouth was opened, and I was no longer mute.*

"Duane," my father-in-law continued, "God sent you to Brenham to deliver a message, and that message was given. He stopped your voice to move you back to Houston and to bring glory to Himself. Ultimately, the new ministry God is going to give to you will far outshine your earlier one."

The sparkle in his eyes made it hard to doubt him. I wanted to believe it was true, but for almost three years, virtually every instance of hope had been a setup for disappointment and a temptation to despair. Just how long can a Christian live on hope alone?

Looking back, I see that though I was emotionally demolished, physically decimated, and spiritually devastated, God knit a family around me who just would not give up: my precious mom, who never stopped telling me I was going to be healed, despite my protests; my wonderful in-laws; my daughter Jodi. They all approached the Throne Room at different times and from different perspectives, but each one of them heard the same voice and the same message: Duane's condition will not be permanent; his voice will be restored.

Can I pause a moment here? I wonder how many readers right now are going through a difficult time. God has been sending you messages of hope and encouragement, but perhaps because you know the messengers so well, you just haven't been able to receive the message. Is that you? Some of you may be feeling the tears building pressure behind your eyes even as you read this. That's okay; let the tears fall on this page. You won't wreck the book—I promise.

Sometimes it's hard to receive encouragement from family members and close loved ones. When life has brought you down to the depths of the pit, however, don't miss God's caress spoken through another human. Listen for His voice in others. God never intended for us to walk this journey of faith on our own.

*Duane Miller*

## HOLDING ON TO FAITH

Back in 1992, in spite of my family's encouragement, I was still struggling. Both Joylene and I knew God could heal. We also continued to hope that He would yet heal *me*. But after almost three years of unanswered prayer, I had become a pragmatist. I felt that it was time to learn to deal with life as it was instead of wasting any more time trying to make it what it could not be. It was just too exhausting to maintain a spirit of expectation.

Finally, one Sunday afternoon, I got on my knees and prayed, "Okay, God, if you choose to change things, which I know you can do—great! But until then, I'm going to accept things as they are and live accordingly."

Ironically, one of my most difficult tests of faith came from witnessing how my ordeal was rocking the faith of others. As a husband, father, and pastor, I have always aimed to draw people nearer to God. The thought that my situation might prove to be a stumbling block to others was a difficult and painful realization.

One such person was Scott, Jodi's boyfriend who eventually became her fiancé (and now her husband). Jodi sometimes tortured him with tales of how I loved to preach and teach and sing, but Scott, understandably, had a hard time imagining it.

One time, when Jodi was away at college, Scott walked up to her apartment and heard an old record before he knocked on the door. It was one that I had recorded some years ago. Jodi missed her father's voice so much that she would listen to "outdated music" just so she could remind herself, "That's my dad. That's what he sounded like."

When Scott asked her about it, Jodi responded, tears welling up around her eyes, "I just needed to hear my father's voice again."

It was understandably painful for Scott to see his sweetheart live with a broken heart. The ground for doubt was fertile.

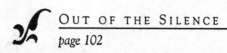

OUT OF THE SILENCE

*page 102*

As Scott's and Jodi's relationship deepened, Scott and I drew closer together as well. When it became obvious that he would soon become my son-in-law, our bond grew even stronger. The closer Scott drew to me, however, the more he began to develop doubts about the reality of the Scriptures. He read about people who had been healed of leprosy and who had been dead but were brought back to life, but if God hadn't changed, he wondered, why wasn't I healed?

Scott would be the son I've never had. He would father (I hope!) my future grandchildren. If ever there was an individual I wanted to pour faith into by the truckload, it was Scott; yet the more time I spent with him, the more he seemed to question the truth of Scripture.

How painful that was! But you know what I've since learned? God is willing to let our faith be "rocked." He's big enough to let us live with doubts for a while, all so that He can prove His faithfulness in ways we could never dream of.

That's what was about to happen to Scott and me. Though my faith would be rocked even more severely in the days ahead, God was stirring up the pot, getting ready to serve the most delicious miracle that Scott or I had ever personally experienced.

# chapter nine

# *Closed
Doors*

SHORTLY BEFORE CHRISTMAS IN 1992, my throat took a turn for the worse. I tried not to let Joylene see what was happening, but one Sunday afternoon when I didn't know she was watching, Joylene saw me slip away and take a sip of water, then recoil from the pain.

"It's getting worse, isn't it?" she asked.

I looked at her precious face and knew it would be pointless to lie. I nodded, and her countenance fell. I walked over to her, hugged her, and led her to the couch.

"We're going to have to prepare ourselves for the day when I can no longer talk at all," I said.

Joylene shook her head. "I can't prepare for that," she insisted. "I just don't know how. If and when it happens, we'll deal with it. But not now."

It was terrifying for me to see my voice slipping. Even though teaching the Catacombs class had become increasingly painful, it was the only hour of the week that I truly enjoyed, and I couldn't bear the thought of watching it slip away.

By this time, the exertion required for me to manufacture a voice was such that I would be wringing wet with sweat after each class. My T-shirt, my dress shirt, and even my suit coat would be drenched, and it became pointless trying to hide this from Joylene. She knew what was coming, I knew what was coming, and there was nothing we could do about it.

Finally, I got up the nerve to broach the subject with Cherie Young. "You know, Cherie," I said, "I think it's time you begin considering other teachers for the Sunday school class."

I wasn't prepared for her adamant, almost angry response. "God told me you're going to teach this class," Cherie insisted. "When He changes His mind, He'll let me know."

I was strangely comforted by this interaction. I didn't want to quit teaching, but I was too tired to maintain hope. More than anything else, I was simply resigned to what was taking place, just waiting for the ugly eventualities to thrust themselves into my life. I had fought this illness, I had fought the loss of my voice, I had fought to find a suitable vocation, I had fought to keep the kids in college, and though I still cared passionately about all these things, I was just exhausted. In many ways, I was saying to myself, "You're gonna hit me again, world? All right, go ahead and hit me."

So when Cherie refused even to consider the demise of my teaching, rather than fight, I just shrugged my shoulders and said, "Fine. I'll go on as long as I can. But you know now, don't you, that I can never guarantee what kind of voice I'll show up with?"

"We'll take care of it, Duane," she assured me.

## INTO THE PIT

On its good months, *Practical Christianity* paid for itself. Mostly, I counted it as an avenue of ministry, not a serious source of income. I had held on to the hope that the government agency would come back, but the prospect of that ever happening had grown increasingly dim with each quiet week. Still, I thought I deserved at least an explanation, so as soon as the Christmas holidays were over, I decided to do a little investigative work of my own.

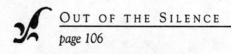

I got hold of one of the guys whom I knew I could trust. He wasn't one of the buck-stops-here guys, but I knew he could find out what I needed to know.

"I was told you were just doing a little reorganizing and that the work would come back," I explained to him. "It's now been over six months, and I haven't received a single assignment. It's obvious I won't get more work from you."

There was absolute silence on the other end.

"Look," I continued, "I just want to know what went wrong. I'm a big boy. If I messed up, I can handle it. I don't care how bad the reason is. I just want to know what happened."

"Fair enough," my friend said. "I'll do a little checking around and see if I can't find out what's going on."

He called back on Friday, January 15, 1993, one of the most difficult days of my life. It was in the morning, I was full of enthusiasm for the new day, and I picked up the phone, eager to hear what he had to say.

"Duane," he said, "I'm almost embarrassed to tell you the truth, but you asked for it so here it is."

I braced myself for his answer.

"I went nosing around a bit and found out what happened last May. Our attorneys went to a management seminar and during the discussion, some of the cases you'd been working on came up. The work you'd done was fine, there was no problem with that, but as the group talked, they become concerned about your ability to testify.

"One of them pointed out that sooner or later you'd have to be put on the stand. Since it would be very difficult for the jury to understand you, the case might be jeopardized, especially since you would be a key witness."

He paused, then added the death blow. "For that reason, and that reason alone, they decided not to use your services anymore."

There was a long moment of silence, after which he added, "I'm sorry for that, but you wanted the truth, and there it is."

*Duane Miller*

I mumbled a perfunctory "thanks" and let the phone drop onto the cradle.

Once again, it was my throat. Always, it seemed, it was my throat. Was it fair? No. But at the same time, I could understand their concern. A high-profile case can cost the government literally millions of dollars to put on. They can't afford to gamble that a key witness wouldn't be able to get his point across. In our legal system, the prosecution gets just one shot at the defendant. If the case is bungled, that's it, it's all over. Guilty or not, the defendant will never be punished.

I understood all this—in a way I could even agree with it—but it still hurt. By "hurt" I don't mean mere disappointment. I was months beyond that stage. By now, the ache had lodged itself deep inside my spirit until the emotional hurt literally became a physical pain. I didn't want to cry. I was tired of crying, and figured it was likely that I had no more tears left.

I dropped my face to my hands and rubbed my eyes, massaging the tears back. It worked. "Well Duane," I said to myself, "you wanted to know, and now you do. Your investigative work is over."

The rest of the day, I did my best to keep a positive outlook. I remembered the book proposals I had sent out about a month ago. I still had that, at least. Surely my throat couldn't stop a *writing* career. Maybe this was just God's way of pointing me in another direction. I had never aspired to be a lifelong private investigator, anyway.

*That's it!* I thought. *God is merely closing one door so that He can open another.*

That afternoon, the mail arrived. The two publishers who had received my proposal managed to respond on exactly the same day.

*This is fantastic,* I thought. *God's timing is amazing. He closes the door in the morning, then opens a new one in the afternoon.*

I tore open the first letter with all the excitement of a child at Christmas, then felt like a sledgehammer thumped me in the chest as the words divulged the sorry truth. Dropping the first letter, I tore open the second one and then fell down onto my chair. At first, it was difficult even to breathe. I just sat there and hurt.

The true agony of the publishers' responses was that their letters were nearly identical. Two people, trained to know their business, had come to the same conclusion. It reminded me of the unanimous opinion of the medical specialists.

Both publishers were brutally honest with me, which I appreciated, but I still felt the anguish of each bitter word. Essentially, the letters read like this:

> *Duane:*
> *Thank you for the submission of your book proposal. It looks commercial and we believe it would sell. It's also very apparent that you have the talent to write. However, because you don't have the name recognition of a Chuck Swindoll or a James Dobson, we would have to put you out on a book tour to promote the book, or at least have you conduct radio interviews. With your voice the way it is, you could never handle a book tour or be understood over the phone for a radio interview. Therefore, though we are very sorry, we will not be able to publish the book for you.*

Both publishers added a harrowing postscript:

> *P.S. We doubt you will find any reputable publisher who will publish your book for you because they will all have the same problem we do. We're really, truly sorry.*

When God closed a door with me, He didn't just gently shut it. Instead, He locked it, deadbolted it, and connected the security chain. There was no way I was going to break through.

I put my head in my hands and tried to get through the pain. I had done my best to hope, but this was really too much to endure. What the publishers were telling me was that my plan "B" had just as many holes as plan "A." Even worse, there

 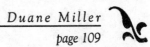

was no plan "C." My swollen, scratchy throat was a black hole swallowing every vocational opportunity I could think of.

I drove home, dazed and emotionally bleeding. People say God never gives us more than we can bear, but that's not in the Scriptures. I was absolutely overwhelmed. It took all my energy to make it up the steps and literally drop myself into a chair in our living room. For some reason, I had hung on to the letters, which now rested in my lap. I put my head back, stared up at the ceiling, and prayed, "God, this isn't funny and it isn't fun. I've had enough. I can't take it anymore, and I'm done. I'm nothing but a burden to my family. Just take me home, because I have nothing left to give and no reason to stay."

An ominous silence filled the room and threatened to suffocate me. I was one giant emotional nerve, hurting, in anguish, alone . . .

*The guns.*

To my horror, I remembered my hunting guns. They looked almost seductive to my mind's eye. I pushed them from my mind, but the thought came racing back.

*The guns.*

They'd provide release. It'd all be over. I wouldn't have to fight any more. God obviously had no use for me here anymore. I was nothing but a burden. My family would be better off without me.

*The guns, the guns, the guns . . .*

In those tense hours, the battle between sanity and suicide was joined. For a few brief moments, sanity would prevail, and I'd chase the ugly thought of self-violence out of my mind, but the seductive lure of suicide was surprisingly strong and would come screaming back at me with its cold, impenetrable logic. I had reached the point of utter despair.

I was sure God had lost my address. I never doubted His sovereignty, but His love and care felt like they were being maliciously withheld. I couldn't shake my fist in God's face and defy Him, but I longed desperately just to feel the tenderness of His touch, a touch that He insisted on withholding. Instead I felt the chasm of emptiness. I was drained of all positive emotion, of all energy, of all enjoyment of life.

I just wanted to surrender, to say, "Okay, that's it, I give up, you win," only I didn't know who the "you" was that I needed to surrender to. Death felt like the only way out.

My voice had been my life. It had provided my greatest pleasure—singing and talking with friends—it represented my livelihood, and now, it represented my only chance at ministry. Its absence signaled the end of my entire world.

I lived that afternoon on the precipice of catastrophe. I don't even want to think about what would have happened if I hadn't known that Joylene would be coming home. The one thought strong enough to overpower the enticement of my guns was the thought of Joylene coming home and finding me.

*I can't do that to her,* I thought, *I just can't.*

But then I'd think, *Maybe she'd be better off without me,* and the debate would start all over again.

Though I never moved from that chair for almost six hours, I don't know that I've ever fought a more intense battle.

Finally, late in the afternoon, I heard Joylene's car pull up. I waited as I heard her unlock the back door and ascend the stairs, which turned and led into the room where I was sitting.

*Poor woman,* I thought, *she has no idea what she's walking into.*

Joylene turned the corner and said in a singsong voice, "What are you doing home so early?"

She looked at me, and the color drained out of her face. "What's wrong, Duane?" She dropped her purse and keys onto the counter and came over to my side.

I handed her the letters from the publishers. Joylene took them from my hands, then sat down on the sofa opposite me and began to read. She laid down the letters, took a deep sigh, and asked, "What does this mean for us?"

I shook my head. "This is it. There's no place left to go."

"You have skills in computers, Duane, you could take some classes and—"

"With what money?"

"What about private investigating? You were good at that."

I explained my morning's conversation.

Joylene and I spent a good thirty minutes talking over options. She was amazing in her creativity, but every time, I'd come back and say, "No, that won't work. That won't work. That won't work . . . "

I had less hope than the Jamaican bobsled team. At least they had a vehicle. All I had was a broken voice that was getting worse.

The next day, Joylene and I stayed away from each other. There was no animosity between us, just a giant wall of frustration and near-despair. The situation was so overwhelming that we couldn't talk about anything else. Since we didn't want to talk anymore about *that*, we simply avoided talking at all. Besides, there was nothing left to say. Neither one of us even hoped to find an answer. We had plumbed the depths looking for one and were quite confident that one didn't exist.

Instead, we poured our energies into cleaning house. There wasn't a single bug, germ, or speck of dust left by 10 P.M.

# chapter ten

# *Surprised
by
God*

I AWOKE ON SUNDAY MORNING
FEELING LIKE I had less to give to an
adult audience than I had ever had in my
entire life. *A first-year Bible college student has more
to say than I do,* I thought. Perhaps because of the
increased stress I was living under, my voice was
noticeably worse and I had more difficulty than
usual manufacturing my raspy whisper. I drank
some tea, hoping that would loosen things up, but
even Joylene flinched when I tested it for the results.

"Duane," she said, "you can't put yourself through this, not
today. Call Cherie and Robert. They'll understand."

I looked at her and knew she was right. Who was I trying
to kid? Not only did I lack the spiritual and emotional strength
to stand up in front of two hundred people, I simply lacked the
physical tools to do it as well. I had warned Cherie about this
day, and now it had come.

*All right,* I thought, *who can I call?* I began rattling off the
names of several individuals in my mind, but everyone was
either busy, out of town, or unavailable. I thought of one or two
other names but wasn't sure how they would do on such short
notice. God had given me such a love for these people that even

in the worst hour of my life, I wouldn't let someone teach the class if I didn't think that person was "qualified."

Looking back, I almost shudder to think what would have happened—or more important, what *wouldn't* have happened—if I had found a replacement. I'm sure God was sovereignly moving at this point, but still, you wonder.

I had no idea God was about to unleash a tremendous miracle. Rather, through seemingly normal events and reasonings, I was unable to locate a substitute. I resigned myself to getting through the class as well as I could, and Joylene and I walked out to the car. We were feeling somber, alone, confused, and hurt.

It's important to point out that when our car pulled out onto the highway and headed toward church, "faith" was about the *last* word I would use to describe my attitude. On the contrary, it was more a *resignation*. I just wanted to fulfill my responsibility and then, quite honestly, come back home and bask in some more self-pity.

In fact, if anything, I went to church with more "show business" than faith. I started my ministry as a professional singer and had learned how to put personal anguish and problems aside when public responsibilities came knocking, and that's what I prepared to do that morning.

Don't be frightened by my use of "show business" when referring to church. Ministry is not an imitation of P. T. Barnum, but my singing career taught me the necessity of having a public persona. On the road, you learn to sing through sickness. Doing so is a part of your "public" responsibility. Certain things are required of you whether you feel good or not. Dates have been set, buildings have been booked, and when the time comes, you must be ready to perform.

As a pastor, I had also learned how to teach through personal trauma. It's not that I'm less than honest, portraying an image of something that isn't there, it's just that people don't come to church to hear about my problems—they come to hear the Word of God. If my current problems can shed light on the gospel, I'll freely share them. If not, I'll keep them to myself.

This is something I've also taught my family. It's part of the maturing process. In the days leading to my daughter Jodi's wedding (after I was healed), Jodi frequently expressed her fear that nobody would show up. That's every bride's nightmare—a white dress, a handsome groom, but an empty church. I assured her she had nothing to worry about, but she couldn't get the thought out of her mind.

As we stood outside the church preparing for the wedding march, Jodi caught a glimpse of the sanctuary through a slightly opened door. The church was certainly not empty! Jodi gasped and started to cry.

"Ah, ah, ah!" I said, stepping forward. "It's show time!"

Jodi composed herself, and we walked down the aisle. She laughed and smiled and lit the room with her radiance.

On the morning of my miracle, I didn't feel like teaching, but I had made a commitment, and now it was time to honor that commitment, so instead of "walking down the aisle," I proceeded to "drive down the road." Spiritually, I was about as low as I have ever been. But I still knew, in the deepest parts of my being, that God's Word was true and worthy of being spoken. I didn't have much of a voice to speak it with, but I'd give Him everything I had.

## RASPY BEGINNINGS

As the two-hundred-plus members filed into the Catacombs class, I managed to greet most of them with a smile and a quick "hello." My eyes surveyed the chapel around me, and I saw some of my oldest and dearest friends getting coffee, popping doughnut holes in their mouths, and shaking hands. They seemed so happy. I knew them well enough to know that many of them faced real problems, but this morning, I envied them. I wondered what it was like to live without overwhelming feelings of hopelessness and despair. I wondered what it must be like to be able to smile spontaneously and to feel good about life, to know that finances were taken care of, to know that you had a job to go to on Monday morning, and to know that, this evening, you could call your kids long distance on the telephone and talk as long as you wanted.

I had been in exactly that position three years ago but never thought twice about it. I lived that life with an almost cavalier attitude, taking work, speech, and financial security for granted.

I greeted one friend, and he melodramatically stepped back when he noticed how raspy my voice was.

"Tell you what, Duane," he said, putting his arm on my shoulder. "Why don't you just tape your notes to your back. I'll stand behind you and read them while you move your mouth. That way, everybody will be better off!"

Now, before you judge this man, understand that we know each other so well that nothing is off limits. I've given more than I've taken, believe me, and on 999 out of 1,000 Sundays, this comment would have made me laugh. Our group had decided long ago that laughter was better than tears when it came to dealing with my malady, so his comments were completely within the good and proper bounds of our relationship.

On this particular morning, however, his words cut through me like sleet driven by a Texas windstorm. I returned a weak smile—he had no way of knowing what my week had been like—and reminded myself of the morning's task. This was the platform God had provided for me to teach His Word, and I needed to be faithful.

*You might not be able to do this for very much longer,* I reminded myself. *Give it your best while you're still able.*

Joylene silently took her seat and tried her best to wear a pleasant expression. A close friend, Cindy Kelley, who was usually involved in another class, came and sat down beside her saying, "I don't know why, but I just thought I should come to Duane's class today. I hope he has something good to share."

Joylene smiled and thought, *If only she knew.*

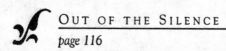

Cherie opened the class with announcements, and we began singing a few songs. We had some special guest singers that morning—ever the able administrator, Cherie had them on cue in case my voice collapsed—and these young people were so good they had even some of us Southern Baptists dancing around! (Figuratively speaking, of course!) Finally, it was my turn to get up and speak.

I stepped up to the small lectern stand and said, "If you have your Bible, please turn to the 68th Psalm and the 103rd Psalm." I winced at the sound of my own voice. It was awful. *How can these people possibly stand to listen to me?* I thought. Well, I was here, the only thing to do was to finish the lesson as quickly as possible. I redoubled my efforts to make my voice carry a little further.

"Isn't God good? It's such a gorgeous day. I think everybody feels good just because the sun's out. I looked outside yesterday and I wasn't sure . . . "

I caught a peek at Joylene as I said those words. Only she knew the sentiment that lay behind them and what a struggle it was for me to say them that morning. I needed to draw on every last second of public speaking experience to put my travail behind me and remind myself as I reminded them, God is good—even when we don't feel like it.

I explained that the introduction to our lesson was from Psalm 68, so we looked at that chapter first. I told the class that the book of Psalms is God's hymnbook, His book of songs.

"You know," I said, "Cherie mentioned that when the singers performed earlier, she hated the fact that she couldn't dance along with them." (Cherie had just undergone surgery on both her feet.)

"Well, one of the things I hated was that I wasn't able to sing along. One of my favorite things to do has always been to worship God in song." (Looking back, I can almost see God begin to smile at this point.)

As we worked our way through the verses, I explained that Psalm 68 is a call to *corporate* worship, an exhortation from King

David to praise the Lord. We proceeded through the lesson until we came to the part relating to God's miraculous and faithful provision for His people.

"Have you ever heard the phrase that the Israelites wandered in the wilderness for forty years?" I asked. "Have you?"

Just about everybody shook their head "yes." That's what I expected.

"This might surprise some of you, but that statement simply isn't true. They weren't wandering. Sure, they may not have known where they were going, but they were following the cloud by day and the pillar of fire by night, both of which represented God's presence. They weren't *wandering*, they were *following*. And God most certainly knew where He was going and where He was taking them. He was never lost and He was never confused. There was a purpose in every step they took, because God *always* has a purpose in everything He does, whether we understand it or not.

"There are times when we follow God and we feel like we are following aimlessly. But when we are following God, there is no aimlessness in it."

Joylene gasped as she listened to me speak. *This is for us*, she thought. *Duane may not be realizing it, but God planned this lesson for us.*

Knowing me so well, however, she made a mental note to get a copy of the tape with the intent of making me listen later on in the week to all the things I was saying this morning. She wanted the physician to heal himself!

I was far from cooperative. I must confess that there was absolutely no great profusion of faith on my part, even at this point. In fact, my words sounded empty and hollow to me. They don't sound that way on the tape, but inside, I was thinking, *What possible purpose could You have for taking my voice, my self-esteem, my ministry? What purpose could it serve for me to be punished as I have been?*

"Do you ever feel like you're by yourself?" I asked the class. "Do you ever feel fatherless? Poor? Do you ever feel like God has forgotten your address, much less your social security number? Do you feel like He doesn't care anymore? Do you feel like He is without power? Do you feel like you're without hope?"

Nobody but Joylene, of course, could know that I was describing how *I* felt. I needed to hear this more than anyone.

"The psalmist tells us that God moved with purpose, and that hasn't changed," I continued. "It's still true today."

I moved down to verse 19. The Bible I was using at the time was the New International Version, which reads, "Blessed be the Lord, Who daily bears our burdens."

"Now," I said, "I prefer the New King James Version for this particular verse, because I believe God does more than just bear our burdens. Does anybody have a New King James Version?"

A member did, and read the words, "Blessed be the Lord, Who daily loads us with benefits."

"God doesn't just bear our burdens," I explained, "He loads us down with benefits!"

I was just minutes away from a tremendously miraculous healing, but all I felt was drudgery. My voice was feeling worse and worse—I began to wonder if I'd even be able to finish the lesson—and it hurt me inside to say what I knew to be true, but didn't feel to be true, that God loads us down with benefits. But heaven itself was beginning to take over, urging me on, leading me toward an incredible manifestation of God's goodness and power.

## BENEFITS

From there we moved to Psalm 103, the heart of the lesson. Here, David becomes much more personal in his approach. He urges his soul and all that is within him to bless the Lord. In Psalm 68, David mentioned how God loads us with benefits, and in Psalm 103, He reminds His soul to not forget a single one:

*Who forgives all your iniquities [sins],*
*Who heals all your diseases,*

*Duane Miller*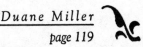

*page 119*

*Who redeems your life from destruction [NIV says "from the pit"],*
*Who crowns you with lovingkindness and tender mercies,*
*Who satisfies your mouth with good things,*
*So that your youth is renewed like the eagle's.*[1]

Forgiveness is the first benefit that David mentions. Almighty God has chosen to forgive my sins—*all* of them. When Jesus hung on the cross some 2,000 years ago, when He bled, died, and was buried, it was to pay the penalty for *my* sins—not His own, certainly, and not just the sins of the disciples or the sins of relatively "good" people, but *my* sins.

I then began talking about the second identifiable benefit—God heals all my diseases. It pains me that such a precious truth has been dragged through the mire and muck of controversy and theological haranguing, but I also understand why it has happened. Like many other pastors, I have been dismayed and embarrassed at the showmanship that often accompanies a "healing ministry." The circus atmosphere, the proven charlatans, the glorification of the minister: we should rightly recoil when confronted with such a distortion.

On the other hand, some conservative evangelicals have developed a systematic theology of dispensations that has left absolutely no room for the miraculous. According to them, I should have lost my voice one or two years ago. The doctors have stated unequivocally that there is no rational, physical explanation for what has occurred in my life. *Somebody* performed a miracle, and I know it wasn't me!

These evangelicals defend their stance by explaining that when the last apostle died the era of miracles ended. They conclude that Christians shouldn't expect God to intervene directly in the lives of men and women today. The proof text they often use is 1 Corinthians 13:8-12:

*Love never fails. But whether there are prophecies, they will fail; whether there are tongues, they will cease; whether there is*

*knowledge, it will vanish away. For we know in part and we*
*prophesy in part. But when that which is perfect has come, then*
*that which is in part will be done away. When I was a child, I*
*spoke as a child, I understood as a child, I thought as a child;*
*but when I became a man, I put away childish things. For now*
*we see in a mirror, dimly, but then face to face. Now I know in*
*part, but then I shall know just as I also am known.*

The argument goes like this: When the Scriptures were completed, that which is "perfect" came. Therefore, we no longer have any need for miracles, prophecies, healings, or any other "gifts of the Spirit," because we have all we need contained in the completed Bible.

You know what this theology reminds me of? It's like putting an eternal God in a time box and telling Him to stay there and behave Himself. Let's face it, few things are more frightening than miracles. We can't make them happen, and we can't stop them from happening. Because of this, we try to tame the tiger by mouthing Christ's powerful words, "Thy will be done," but in the back of our minds we are saying, "But please don't do anything we can't explain in natural terms."

The one thread holding my life together—from the time the ink dried on my birth certificate until the day a chisel carves out my name on a tombstone—is without question a strong belief in the sovereignty of God. God placed me with the parents He chose for me. I was born in the exact time I needed to be born in. I caught the flu the exact minute God knew I'd catch it. When my voice disintegrated, it did so only after passing through the permissive will of Almighty God.

While I have great respect for the way dispensationalists shed light on how God has worked and continues to work with man, I must part ways with them when it comes to limiting His healing. Otherwise, my entire life would be a lie. I don't know why God "jumped out of His time box" to heal me, but He did, and it would be silly for me to deny it.

*Duane Miller*

It's not just the dispensationalists I take issue with, however, but also the "hyper-healers" who insist that *everyone* will be healed of *every* disease *every* time because Jesus died on the cross. I'm sure you've met a proponent of this view. They say things like, "My God not only *can* heal, He *will* heal, if I pray in faith." When somebody doesn't get well, the hyper-healer insists that there must be some buried sin or perhaps a sliver of "unbelief" blocking the flow of God's provision.

If sinless perfection and heroic faith were prerequisites of healing, believe me, I'd have taken up sign language a long time ago. There's no way I'd be healed.

The hyper-healers' proof text is Isaiah 53:5: "By His stripes we are healed." The problem with using this verse to insist that God will always heal is that the context is clearly referring to spiritual restoration. To impress physical healing as the only meaning of the passage is to do violence to the context of God's Word.

I would also remind my brothers and sisters who hold to this view that Scripture clearly states that God *wills* that not "any should perish but that all should come to repentance."[2] However, any orthodox Christian is going to agree that not everyone will be saved; some will be lost.

In many ways, I'm a man without a theological country. I don't fit in the dispensationalist camp, because I believe that God can and does heal today. I don't fit in the hyper-healers camp, because I also know that sometimes God chooses not to heal. The morning my voice was restored, a young man, thirty-eight years old, was sitting in the congregation. He had two lovely kids, and one ugly brain tumor. Our class had poured out many prayers on his behalf. Two weeks after my voice came back, this young man died.

Why? Why would God's Spirit reach into my throat, literally rebuild it and make it new, and then bypass such a promising young man who had such young dependents? This young man loved God as much as I did. Why wasn't he healed?

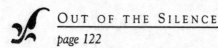

The only answer I can give you is, "Beats me." I don't know. I don't know why God chose to heal me, and I don't know why God chose not to heal that young man. It's a mystery, and our modern, self-satisfied theological systems often have precious little space for mystery.

One thing I do understand, however, is the indisputable meaning of Psalm 103:3. It means exactly what it says: "God heals all my diseases." However, as we explore this verse, we must not attempt to define the infinite in finite terms. The young man who had the brain tumor *was* healed. Today, the tumor is no longer a part of his existence. But God chose to heal it with *death*. Sometimes, God chooses to heal with life, "loaning" His beloved another several decades to enjoy the beauty and manage the responsibilities of time on earth; at other times, He takes His beloved into His heaven. Always, it's His choice.

So that morning I made it very clear that the Almighty is neither a "genie-in-a-bottle" nor an apathetic bystander who no longer gets involved. Please don't ask me to choose sides, because I think both positions generate more theological heat than theological light. If less time and effort were spent in being right, and more in being compassionate, the kingdom would be benefited greatly.

Ironically and prophetically, I asked the class, "What happens when we put God in a box and say He doesn't heal anymore?" I paused for maximum effect. "He kicks all the walls down."

God was putting on His boots.

## OUT OF THE PIT

When I listen to the tape of that teaching now, I have to smile at the incongruity of a man who had clearly lost his voice affirming to his fellow Southern Baptists that God still heals today. The irony didn't escape me back then either, even on stage. With my tongue, I was saying, "I still believe that God heals," but in my heart I was screaming, *But why not me, Lord? Why haven't you healed me?*

It was more of an accusation than a prayer. I want to obliterate any sense of the notion that I did anything at all to earn or unleash what was about to take place. My faith did not "grow" here; resignation still carried the day, even though God was about to slay me with His kindness.

To the class I added, "We have to be careful here. God doesn't intend that healing become a show. God heals in His sovereign will. I don't know why God does the things that He does, but I know that He does. The only thing He requires of me is to allow Him to be God and me to be me, and let it be."

I had to add this statement. How could I, with a seriously damaged, "false" voice, who had been the object of so many prayers, face these people and say, "God heals"? Only because God's Word said it.

I went on to Psalm 103:4, which reads (in the NIV), "he redeems my life from the pit."

Now, I thought, finally, a part of the passage I could understand! I knew pits, believe me! I had been swallowed by my pit. It had been days since I had seen the dawn of hope's burgeoning light. To this day, I could tell you what the pit tastes like (bitter) and what it looks like (a darkness that swallows all the other colors around it).

I understood pits like few people ever have, so I prepared myself to really let the Sunday school class have it. The part on benefits and healing were offered because I knew they were true, even though experientially I wasn't feeling them. But pits, well, I could really put my heart into pits, because I was in one.

I got ready to speak for several minutes when God opened up a window in heaven and struck down more than two hundred members of the Catacombs class with a display of His power that still makes my knees shake and the hair on the back of my neck rise when I think about it.

## LOOSED!

My throat hurt very badly at this point. I had been teaching for over twenty minutes, and I had to strain especially hard to make even the raspy sound come out. I wondered if I'd be able to finish the class. After reading verse four, I began saying, "I have had and you have had in times past *pit* experiences."

As soon as the word "pit" escaped from my mouth, the hands that had been choking my throat for over three years suddenly let go. I was stunned. Just seconds before, I felt like I was suffocating under the pressure of those unrelenting hands. Now, for the first time in three years, I could breathe.

I heard a gasp in the crowd, and that's when I, too, realized my voice had come back. I could hear myself! Still not quite believing what was taking place, I said a few more words. My speech was halting at this point—out of shock more than anything else—but my resonance was clear. At first, I was afraid that maybe this would be another false alarm, but the incredibly free sensation in my throat told me this was about more than having a voice—I had a new throat!

"We've all had times when our lives have seemed to be in a pit, in a grave," I went on, speaking with an absolutely, positively normal voice. My voice was there, it was clearly there! I stopped again, too stunned to go on, then spoke once more, and my voice was still there!

Still, I asked myself, *Is that what I think it is?* It sounded like my voice, it felt like my voice, it was coming from my mouth, but the best doctors in the world had told me I'd never have a voice again.

As I spoke, I could feel sensations around my Adam's apple that I hadn't felt for three long years. What was dead had literally and stunningly come back to life. On the tape, you can hear my voice quiver, not from weakness but from emotion. I had grown to despise and hate the sound of my false voice, in part because of all the things it represented—no ministry, no vocation, no singing. To be delivered from that horrendous sound felt like a peasant being delivered from a harsh and sadistic taskmaster. It was a freedom that filled me to the depths of my soul.

Joylene gripped Cindy's arm and said, "Listen to his voice!" She saw me look at her, and she began crying. It was a shout, really, a spontaneous explosion of disbelief, joy and utter thankfulness. The first thing Joylene thought was, *Now he'll be able to sing!* It had been so very long since she had heard her husband's real voice, and now she ran to me like an Olympic runner chasing a gold medal.

I was so overcome that I didn't even realize Joylene was next to me. The class reacted with cheers and shouts and laughter and tears, and my restored voice broke with emotion.

"I don't understand this right now," I said. "I'm overwhelmed at the moment. I'm not quite sure what to say or do. I'm—I know this sounds funny to say—I'm at a loss for words."

The class erupted into laughter and cheers once again.

"Thank you, Lord," I said, still amazed and delighted that I could feel and hear my own voice.

## OVERWHELMED

Had anything like this ever happened before? Had God ever broken into the middle of a Southern Baptist Sunday school class and unveiled His glory with such strength?

The presence of the Holy Spirit was so palpable that everyone's nerve endings felt exposed. It was as if we were lifted to a higher existence and you could take hold of the Spirit with your bare hands. There was an electricity in the air that elicited different reactions from different members. Some dropped to their knees and prayed. Others cried. A few danced like children in their joy.

Everywhere and for everyone, colors became more vibrant. Sounds, voices, and the music seemed to take on a new life.

Joylene felt like she was being carried by the river of the Holy Spirit. At times it surrounded and submerged her. It was all like a wonderful, wonderful dream.

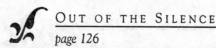

For my part, I felt like Lazarus must have felt. God had given me my life back. I wanted to laugh, cry, sing, shout, dance, and hug everybody I could, all at the same time. After a few brief moments, I thought, what better way to celebrate the restoration of my voice than by teaching God's Word? So I attempted to go on with the lesson.

Later, people would tell me how surprised they were that I could continue to teach so soon after the miracle occurred—but I was surprised—absolutely amazed—at how well the rest of the passage I was reading fit together with what was happening. It was like God had planned everything in advance. I skipped around a bit as I read, almost like a child at play, joyfully landing on those phrases that seemed to showcase what God was doing right then.

"'He redeems my life from the pit,'" I went on, occasionally laughing as I spoke, "'and crowns me with love and compassion. He satisfies my desires with good things, so that my youth is renewed like the eagle's. The LORD works righteousness and justice for all the oppressed. . . . The LORD is compassionate and gracious . . . '

"That's mercy!" I added. "Or repay us according to our iniquities. For as high as the heavens are above the earth, so great is his love for those who fear him; as far as the east is from the west, so far has he removed our transgressions from us."

At this point, my tears made further talk impossible. I was so overcome by God's goodness and by the truth of these Scriptures that it was impossible to go on.

Finally, I said, "I'm sorry for the emotions," but then I realized, I really wasn't. So I corrected myself. "No, I'm not! That's a lie." We all laughed together. "I'm not. I wish I could let you see how I feel inside right now. I wish I could see how I feel inside right now. Oh, bless the Lord! Bless the Lord! Bless the Lord!"

The room broke into spontaneous applause once again. It was almost impossible *not* to bless the Lord.

*Duane Miller*

I thought about going on but realized it would be impossible. The miracle had restored my voice but reduced my logic and clear thinking to mush. Imagine having a million volts of electricity rip through your body and then trying to put two coherent words together. That's how I felt! I had a tremendous amount of emotion pushing against my insides, begging to be let out, but I didn't know *how* to do so.

"I don't think I can stay with the structure, guys," I said. "I've lost my thought. I've lost it. It's gone."

But my voice was back!

"Let me just wrap it up by saying this," I went on. "I know that wherever you are in your life and whatever is going on with you, and however deep the pit or however high the mountain, God is there! He is there! And as you have lived with me these last years—would you believe, three years this Sunday, three years today since I preached my last sermon . . . "

This sudden realization took all my strength away. I cried tears of pure joy and overwhelming gratitude.

Dave Patterson, who was responsible for music in the class, stood up and began to sing the doxology. It was a perfect addition, and everyone soon joined him.

*Praise God from whom all blessings flow! Praise Him all creatures here below! Praise Him above ye heavenly hosts. Praise Father, Son, and Holy Ghost!*

The words came alive in a new way. I don't think anybody who was there that day will ever again sing the doxology in a casual manner. The truth of its simplicity struck our hearts for eternity.

I had more than a new voice. God had given me a new life. It was like being born again *again!*

# chapter eleven

# *Duane
Is
Healed!*

A T FIRST, CHERIE YOUNG DIDN'T REALIZE what was going on. She was busy being the administrator and taking attendance while I taught. In fact, before she heard my voice, she heard Joylene crying and looked up to see what was wrong. (Because Cherie is a close friend, Joylene had confided in her earlier about how depressed I was, so Cherie's immediate thought was that the teaching was just too close to home. Joylene had finally broken.)

Ever wanting to comfort the hurting, Cherie put down her papers and rose. It was then that she heard my voice and gasped. Her surprise faded into tears of disbelief and then joy. Once the class was over, Cherie was out the door as fast as her orthopedic shoes would carry her. Cherie was recovering from surgery on both feet, but neither Carl Lewis nor Emmitt Smith would have been able to outsprint her that day!

She ran toward Dr. Bisagno's office, yelling, "Duane is healed! Duane is healed!" One of the associate pastors stopped her.

"What's going on?" he asked.

"Duane's been healed!" she said, still rushing forward.

"Oh, that's why I just saw a woman crying!" he said.

Cherie, still in a hurry, shot back over her shoulder, "Any woman who walks into the sanctuary without her eye makeup on was in our class! Believe me!"

As Cherie drew near, Brother John came out of his office to see what was the matter. He found Cherie out of breath and weeping, her face covered with tears. Now, John is a large man—6-foot-3—and his arms completely enveloped Cherie as he asked, "Cherie, what's wrong? Is it Robert?"

Cherie, flustered, shook her head.

"Is it the boys?"

Cherie shook her head and held up her hands. She wanted to tell him—she was bursting—but she was too excited.

"It's Duane," she finally managed to get out. "It's Duane. He's been healed. He has his voice back!"

"His *real* voice?" Brother John asked.

"Yes!"

"What happened?"

Dr. Bisagno was about to go on live (our services are broadcast on the radio and recorded for a later broadcast on television), so Cherie knew she had to hurry. She gave him a three-sentence summary of what had taken place.

And here's the next miracle. This wonderful pastor believed her—in spite of the fact, as Cherie loves to recount, that he was fully aware Cherie's foot surgery had her taking pain-killing drugs. Brother John had seen many, many healings during various crusades, so God had prepared him. I believe he has what the New Testament calls the "gift of faith." Later, someone would ask him if he was surprised, and his answer was, "Not at all. As a pastor, I live in a world of miracles and see them all the time. However," he added, winking, "this one was a little more dramatic than most."

"Go get him," Brother John told Cherie. "Tell him I want him on the platform with me right now."

Because our services are recorded, they must be scripted, literally by the second. Who sits on the platform, who speaks and for how long, what the order of service is, all has to be carefully and meticulously laid out ahead of time. When Brother John made a last-minute—no, a last-*second* change—he was risking sending the producer into absolute mutiny! But both Dr. Bisagno and I were to learn that day that God has a way of overturning schedules.

## A NEW PLATFORM

Since the healing, some people have asked me if I ever feared I'd lose my voice again. What if, they asked, this was another "false start" like the one that had occurred a year earlier? Here I was, about to go on both television and radio, and talk about a healing. Was I scared that it might not last?

There's a quick answer for that. It never even crossed my mind. This healing was so dramatically different from the previous remission that there really was no comparison. Back then, I got a *version* of my voice back, but it never sounded the same. And my throat still felt like it was full of stuffing. This morning, that awful and bothersome pressure had been completely obliterated.

Even more important, however, is that for the first time in three years I was able to speak without manufacturing a voice. I didn't have to think about making sounds come out. Because I had my real vocal cords back, the words left my throat effortlessly. I felt great, and it never occurred to me that I wasn't absolutely, 100 percent healed.

The news had traveled through the church even faster than gossip, so I was soon surrounded by excited well-wishers and jubilant friends. Cherie elbowed her way through the crowd and came up to me.

"Brother John wants you on the platform," she said. "You have to go, *now.*"

Like Cherie's word *retrieved*, spoken during a difficult and trying time, her phrase, *on the platform*, also spoke to me. For three years, my platform had been taken away. For three years,

I felt like God had dug a hole, put me in it, and then covered me up with His hand.

Now, I was about to go live on radio, of all things. My new voice would be carried out to thousands of homes. God was giving me a new platform.

Immediately I began to be pulled along, heading toward the sanctuary, when I realized that I had been separated from Joylene. Crowds of people had surrounded us both and unwittingly cut us off from each other. I looked around to find her, but I couldn't even see her.

"What about Joylene?" I asked Cherie.

"I'll get Joylene," she answered. "You go, *now.*"

By the time I reached the sanctuary, the service had already begun. The television cameras were already rolling, the lights were on, and the choir was singing. Brother John met me at the top step, grabbed me by the shoulders, and said, "All right Preacher, talk to me!"

For a split second, the thought went through John's mind, *"What if he's not really healed? I've got him up on stage!"* Keep in mind that our service has to run like a well-oiled machine. When a deacon is told he has thirty-eight seconds to make an announcement, that means thirty-eight seconds, not thirty-nine. Yet Brother John was preempting all of that, and he hadn't even talked to me!

"Praise the Lord, Preacher!" I said.

Tears poured down my pastor's face like rain on a windowpane. Brother John had prayed with me and wept with me and agonized with me (as only a fellow pastor could) over the fact that my ministry was compromised because of my illness. When he heard my voice, his joy overflowed from deep within his soul and flooded his eyes with tears. He embraced me, and motioned for me to sit down beside him.

I looked out over the congregation and saw Joylene in the front row and started weeping. I was so happy for her, for *us.* She had been so faithful as a wife.

The church was packed. Word had gotten around so quickly that many people who had attended the first service came back for the second. People were standing by the walls, eager, excited, and exhilarated by the news.

The sound of the choir was nothing less than angelic. John kept leaning over every couple of minutes, telling me, "Say something else. I just want to hear you say something else."

I laughed and said, "Isn't God good?"

"Are we having fun yet?"

"What a day to praise God!"

Each time I spoke, it was like turning John's faucet back on. He'd begin crying again, and we both looked like children in our happiness.

I was deeply touched that this giant man was as genuinely excited by my healing as he would have been had it happened to him. In Brother John's eyes, I saw the true love of Christ, shining out and making his face radiant.

The first break in the service finally arrived. Brother John leaned over yet again and said, "Okay, Duane, I want you to come to the pulpit."

We both stood up and approached the pulpit. Dr. Bisagno spoke first. "Folks, most of you in this room know Duane Miller because he's been around the church for the best part of twenty years now, except when he was pastoring in Brenham. And most of you know the struggle he's had with his voice the last three years. I want him to come and tell you what God is doing in his life."

I was no stranger to this pulpit. I had dissected and taught God's Word on this very spot. The sight of the sanctuary was so familiar to me that I could close my eyes and picture virtually every distinguishing mark on the walls by memory.

I had also addressed this congregation for what seemed like a thousand times. They knew me well. They had heard me preach many times over. Even so, my knees were weak and my hands were shaking as I gripped the brass pulpit for what little support it could provide. I wasn't afraid of the people, but the power of God was so intense that I could hardly stand in His presence. I was so overwhelmed with His holiness and goodness that it seemed impossible not to throw myself on the floor and bask in His wonderful presence.

When Brother John motioned to me, I somehow managed the strength to step forward and say, "Well, I'll try . . . "

That's as far as I got. The entire sanctuary erupted! God got a sustained standing ovation. People came to their feet and began to applaud—on and on for two to three minutes, which in the midst of a broadcast church service is a very, very long time. Tears flowed freely as I thanked God for creating such a joy in His people. Finally, the congregation began to quiet down. In halting speech, I tried to explain what was going on in my soul and my spirit, but it was so new and so fresh and so marvelous that I was speechless to describe the beauty that was holding me.

Joylene felt the same way. A woman sitting next to her, whom Joylene didn't even know, reached out and took her hand. The symbolism was powerful. One hour ago, we felt like we had completely run out of options. Now, we had more choices than we knew how to deal with, and comfort was coming from people we didn't even know!

Joylene was reminded of a missionary family that we had treated by taking them out to a buffet restaurant. The kids were so stunned by the vast array of choices that they went all the way through the service line without choosing a single item! Both of their trays were empty. They just weren't used to having so many options, and they couldn't make up their minds!

I felt like someone leaving a dark theater in the middle of a brilliantly sunny afternoon. You step outside, and all of a sudden it feels like the light is reaching into the back of your eyes and blinding you. The onslaught is so great that you're too stunned to do anything besides wait for your eyes to adjust. That's what I had to do. My spiritual eyes had to adjust to the blinding light.

*I'm alive again,* I thought. I wasn't thinking about vocation, finances, or anything that weighed so heavily on my shoulders the day before. Instead, I was just reveling in the resurrection experience. It was so powerful that I finally said, "I just don't know what to say or how to say it."

John broke in and said, "Well, we do!" He looked at the organist, and as if on cue, began to lead us in that beloved Bill Gaither song, "Let's Just Praise the Lord." *Let's just praise the Lord, praise the Lord, let's just lift our hearts toward heaven, and praise the Lord . . .*

I joined in. It was unbelievably beautiful for me to sing again. For three years, my most precious form of worship had been cut off. My most satisfying recreation had been taken away. But now it came back in full force. My throat moved and vibrated just as it should, and the sounds coming from my throat were so beautiful to me that I wept as I sang.

The congregation was on its feet again, laughing, crying, singing, raising their hands to heaven in praise and worship. More than two dozen people came to the altar and gave their lives to Christ on the spot. Joylene was smothered with well-wishers. God's love filled the room.

One of the most beautiful aspects of my healing is that it was a miracle given not just to an individual but to a community. This church had shared our anguish, wept many tears on our behalf, sent us to Brenham, retrieved us, helped us find a new vocation, stood with me as we formed the board for *Practical Christianity*—they had walked through the entire ordeal with us. Though we were often hurting, we were never alone.

As Christians, we hear about healings on television all the time, but this church could say, "This one's real. We know this one. We experienced it."

After several minutes, Dr. Bisagno finally brought order back to the service. Deacons took the newly converted to another room for additional discussion, and our pastor began his sermon.

I deserved an Oscar for my performance that morning. As Dr. Bisagno preached, I nodded my head and looked at him like I was hanging on to every word he said. I knew I was on television and I wanted to support my brother and pastor. But in reality, I didn't have a clue what he was saying. The reality of what had just occurred began to descend on me, and I understood for the first time just how much had changed. Like Lazarus, I was a dead man who had come back to life. I was floating with joy.

After Dr. Bisagno was done preaching, he gave another invitation, and once again, people made their way to the altar. It was a tremendous response.

Let's not forget that these decisions for Christ were even more significant than my own healing. God had changed my life for the next several decades, but He changed these new Christians' lives for the rest of eternity. My voice was restored, but their destiny was secured!

My appreciation for my pastor and his wise leadership grew. He perceived that God had opened a window, and he used that opening to help populate heaven, as a wise pastor should.

This experience has taught me to be very uncomfortable when I hear of situations where miracles squeeze out the proclamation of the Word. This is dangerous for several reasons, but the primary reason is that only the Word of God has an eternal effect. True, miracles can bless believers and seize the attention of unbelievers, but unless they are followed up by disciplined teaching and the careful application of the Word of God, there will be no lasting change, even in those who experience the miracles firsthand.

## SPREADING THE GOOD NEWS

"I can't *believe* you did this to me," Cherie's husband, Robert, complained. During Sunday school and the second service, Robert was in the Christian Life Center donating blood. The Christian Life Center has a PA system that broadcasts the

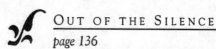

church service, so he heard what had happened over the airwaves.

"What?" I asked in disbelief.

"I was giving blood! I missed it! How *dare* you get healed when I wasn't in the room!"

I laughed, and we hugged, and I thought, *Everyone who gets healed should have such a wonderful group of people to share it with!*

After church, Joylene and I were surrounded by people who shared our joy. We cried so long and so hard and so frequently that it's a wonder we weren't dehydrated. It took us forever to get out of there; nobody was in a hurry to leave that afternoon, so I'm sure there were a lot of bored waitresses, wondering where all the business was.

Joylene and I were like a couple of newlyweds, delighted to have our dearest and closest friends share our joy, but eager to leave the reception and enjoy an even deeper intimacy. In this case, we couldn't wait to tell our daughters and family.

Finally, we were in our van and headed for home. As we stepped inside our house—the house of our sorrow, the house of my despair, the house that almost witnessed a desperate act of suicide—we erupted into spontaneous joy. We hugged and cried in the living room, spending some time in prayer thanking God not just for this wonderful, delightful healing, but for the friends, church, and pastor with whom we were able to share it.

Joylene and I gushed as we planned the calls to Jodi and Lisa. We called Lisa first. Joylene, making the call as always, asked to speak to Lisa. Her roommate went to get Lisa, and I slipped onto the phone and said, "Hello."

"Who is this?" Lisa demanded.

"It's me, Punkin," I said, using my pet name for her, and Lisa erupted into shouts and tears of joy.

We repeated the same scenario for Jodi.

"Hello," I said, teasingly.

"Who is this?" Jodi wanted to know. She figured it had to be me, because I was the only man her mom would be with, but the possibility of that seemed so remote that her mind was in utter confusion.

"It's me, Peanut."

Jodi became so hysterical that she ran over to Scott's apartment and actually fell at his feet. (Scott jokes that this was miracle number two, and that it will never happen again. Jodi assures him he's right!) From the way Jodi was reacting, Scott thought that somebody in our family had died. It took Jodi several minutes to collect herself sufficiently to tell him I had been healed.

Jodi was a freshman when I first got the flu that eventually took away my voice, so my silence took her through the bulk of her college experience. When she heard that my voice was restored and she went to tell her sorority sisters the good news, the first thing they said was, "We've got to have him back."

When I was healed and the Zetas asked me back, we had a tremendous celebration. Literally hundreds of young women had been aware of and prayed for my condition for three years—which at that age was actually a significant chunk of their life. After I was finished speaking, one of the women asked me to sing. They had heard Jodi's records, and though at first I declined, they persisted, and I eked out a little tune.

It was through one of the Zetas that I began to get an understanding of just how far news of this healing had traveled and gain my first inkling of how God was going to use it to build up His entire church. One of the Zetas returned home that summer and heard her pastor recount my story. After his sermon, she went up to him and said, "I know the man you're talking about! His daughter is a fellow Zeta, and he spoke to us."

After our daughters, of course, I called my mother. She was the one who had always told me I'd be healed, even when I didn't care to hear it anymore. I wished I didn't have to tell her over the phone. I wanted to put my arms around her and softly tell her what had happened. But she deserved to know as soon as possible, and she would have disowned me if I had made her wait.

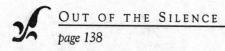

OUT OF THE SILENCE

"Hi, Mom," I said.

"Who is this?" (I was beginning to wonder if this response was genetically programmed into the female side of the Millers.) I wanted to laugh. My mother has only one child. If somebody was calling her "Mom," it had to be me—but she just wasn't expecting to hear my voice.

"You really don't know, do you?" I asked gleefully.

"The voice is familiar," she said, "I just can't place it."

My mother started getting exasperated as I continued to tease her, so finally I said, "Fine thing, you don't even recognize your son's voice."

She laughed, she cried, she shouted. And then she, too, began subsidizing the long-distance phone services with accounts of the great news.

Joylene called our cousins and asked them to come over. "Duane needs to see you," she said.

As soon as they walked in the door, they said, "Duane has his voice, doesn't he?" They had no earthly way of knowing this, but God's Spirit was already proclaiming the good news.

We called Joylene's parents, who were on a mission trip to Kenya. They were staying in a rural area that had just one phone. Our first call was simply to inform the people that we wished to speak with the Corrells (Joylene's parents). We said we'd call back in about twenty minutes.

Dad came to the phone and waited nervously. He knew we wouldn't go to the trouble of reaching him out there unless it was vitally important. Even though he had to wait just twenty minutes, he said, it was an agonizing wait.

When he finally heard my voice, he broke into tears of rejoicing. This godly man could fully appreciate all that God had done for us. We talked, we laughed, we cried, we thanked God together.

Being able to use the phone to communicate with my dearest loved ones was such a delightful treat. It was overwhelming to carry on a conversation. Scott, who would one day be my son-in-law, had never heard my voice before. He called me later in the day, and we had the first of our many meaningful (and long-winded) conversations over the phone.

As soon as Joylene's dad got off the phone, he went to tell her mom the news, but God upstaged him.

"Sit down!" he said. "I have some news for you."

"Duane has been healed!" she gushed. She already knew in her spirit that God had answered her petition.

"Yes! Yes! It's true! It's true!"

Some family and friends gathered that afternoon for an informal celebration. After the phone calls and a bite to eat (it was absolute *ecstasy* to swallow without pain after teaching for an hour), I actually sat down and watched a race on television.

"How can you do that?" somebody asked.

I was so overwhelmed, I just needed a point of escape to gather my thoughts. Twelve hours ago, the entire world had been shut off. Now, I felt like the doors had burst open and the world had just been born! It was too much! I needed a reprieve!

## THE AFTERMATH

As much as it meant to me personally to have my voice restored, it was also a blessing to realize how God's name was being lifted up because of what had happened. Now, people in Kenya who had never heard of me were thanking God for the miracle He had wrought. People in Houston had become Christians and were living their first few hours as children of God. The phone lines were buzzing with the news, and everywhere people were shouting, "Praise the Lord!"

The miracle didn't just bless *me*. It blessed thousands of people who had come in contact with me, and I took just as much satisfaction in that as I did in having my voice restored. Even on that afternoon, I had no way of knowing the difference this one miracle would make in the kingdom of God—that literally tens of thousands would eventually believe on the name of Jesus.

I didn't understand—and I still don't—how God put everything together. God's Word puts it more eloquently than I can:

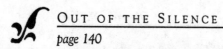

"Oh, the depth of the riches both of the wisdom and knowledge of God! How unsearchable are His judgments and His ways past finding out!"[1]

But I do know this: Even when the pain of my ordeal eclipsed my ability to feel God's love, His love was still there. The loss of my voice and the pressure in my throat couldn't suffocate the fact that Jesus died for me.

As I learned so dramatically on Sunday morning, January 17, 1993, no "pit experience" lasts forever. Sooner or later, one way or another, God will break through and the light will shine again.

Some of the people reading this may have a hard time believing that. "My ordeal has lasted longer than three years!" some of you might be saying. "Why hasn't God healed *me?*"

I can't answer that. I can't give you "ten principles to prepare for God's healing." It wasn't my faith, it wasn't my response, it wasn't my obedience. I didn't earn a thing, I didn't do a thing. I just received His unearned favor.

Eventually, however, your pit experience will end—the real pit experience, that is, which is the pit experience of sin. Maybe your physical body won't be healed until heaven. But the day will come when, like me, light will flood your soul and your trial will melt away and suddenly, you'll be free again.

That's not my promise, that's *His* promise, and God *keeps* His promises.

# An Unusual Doctor's Appointment

ON TUESDAY, I CALLED MY MEDICAL team with a real air of triumph. The doctors were incredulous when they heard about my healing, and they wanted to see me right away. I have to confess, I particularly enjoyed the amazement that spread across my attending physician's face when he heard me speak. By now, I felt like he and I had become more than doctor and patient. We had spent so much time together that a true friendship had begun to develop.

He sat me down and began running a series of tests. I was used to this, but it felt new. I had to fight back the tears when I realized that for the first time these doctors were running tests to figure out what went *right* rather than what went wrong.

My physician spent an inordinate amount of time on the videotapes of my throat. I watched him running the earlier ones, spliced with the recent one, over and over again.

"What's going on, Doctor?" I asked.

"This is your throat before," the doctor said, running a clip of videotape, "and this is your throat now."

I flinched when I looked at the ugly scarring that marred the earlier videos, then felt my own eyes open wide when we came to the new clip and I saw the smooth surface that had taken its place.

"Not only are you okay," he said, "but I can't find any evidence that you ever had a voice problem!"

He sat down and looked at me, amazed. "Even if I could explain how you got your voice back by coincidence—which I can't—I could never explain what happened to the scar tissue." He sighed. "Scar tissue *never* disappears. It just never happens!"

This physician, a nonbeliever so far as I know, was so impressed that he eventually obtained hundreds of copies of the audiotape of when the healing occurred and sent them out to his friends and colleagues with a letter that said, "Look, we hear about these types of cases all the time, but I'm telling you, I witnessed this one, I have the test evidence. This one is *real*."

My doctor writes textbooks for medical schools. He specializes in neurology as it relates to speech—and he personally verified the miracle with the most prestigious of his colleagues. It didn't take me long to realize that God was going to get a lot of glory out of this miracle.

Imagine, to get to the point of my healing, the medical professionals who received the tape from my doctor must first endure a verse by verse exposition of Psalm 68 and Psalm 103. They're going to hear about the sovereign God who offers to heal all their diseases and forgive all their sins!

As I left his office, amazed at his words—"Scar tissue *never* disappears"—it was as if a light went on and I finally understood what my healing was all about. Right there in the middle of the medical district I wanted to shout, jump up, and click my heals.

I remembered the 103rd Psalm—that God heals all my diseases and forgives all my sins. Our sins are ugly scars that stay with us through eternity—unless, that is, Jesus comes in and completely removes them.

*I'm a living illustration of forgiveness.*

The thought hit me in such a dramatic and clear way that I just stood there, stunned. The point of last Sunday was not

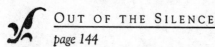

just my healing, I realized, but a living parable of God's desire to forgive, to remove the scar tissue of sin and self and remake us into entirely new beings. Today, my throat looks like it never had a problem—but anybody who knew me five years ago knows that I had one of the worst throat problems in medical history.

In the same way, God can take a sin-stained soul and remake it into the very image of love and wholeness. He can remove those ugly scars—the dreaded habits, temptations, and character flaws—and replace them so thoroughly and completely that we become new spiritual creatures.

This connection between healing and forgiveness isn't limited to my own experience. Have you ever noticed that every time Jesus healed someone, He did so for the purpose of demonstrating that He could forgive sin? Take Mark 2 for instance. Jesus looks upon a paralytic and doesn't say, "Be healed." Instead, He says, "Son, your sins are forgiven you."

WHAT? The scribes were thrown into near apoplexy just moments after Jesus' words escaped from his mouth. DID HE SAY "YOUR SINS ARE FORGIVEN"??? HOW DARE HE!

Jesus turned to the scribes and chided them for making God's simplicity so incredibly confusing.

> "Why do you reason about these things in your hearts? Which is easier, to say to the paralytic, 'Your sins are forgiven you,' or to say, 'Arise, take up your bed and walk?' But that you may know that the Son of Man has power on earth to forgive sins"— He said to the paralytic, "I say to you, arise, take up your bed, and go your way to your house."[1]

Well, if you were the paralytic, what would you do? Side with the Pharisees and refuse to be healed, or jump up and take your chances? We don't have to guess. Mark tells us: "Immediately [the paralytic] arose, took up the bed, and went out in the presence of them all, so that all were amazed and glorified God, saying, 'We never saw anything like this!'"[2]

Notice the crowd's response. They were amazed, so what did they do? They glorified God. The physical restoration pointed them toward their ultimate spiritual need. That's exactly what happened after my healing. Amazement set in, and then people began praising and glorifying God.

It's because some sectors of the church teach healing as largely a "feel good" proposition that evangelicals have overreacted and devalued its impact. Because we're so afraid of being labeled charismatic or Pentecostal, we don't even pray for people. And yet, as our church discovered, healing can have an enormous impact on a church's witness and evangelism.

I now go to the doctors every six months. They want to track me for the rest of my life, and after all they've done for me, I'm happy to oblige. I still get new confirmation from these meetings, anyway. When a new doctor examined me recently, he said something that puzzled me.

"Are you an accountant?" he asked.

"Absolutely not," I laughed.

"Well, you don't use your voice much, do you?"

"You've got to be kidding me," I said. "I've preached over two hundred times during the past twelve months."

The doctor was astonished. "Your throat looks like an accountant's. It shows none of the wear and tear of a professional speaker."

Do you have any idea how excited that makes me? God didn't just repair my throat—he remade it, cell by cell.

## HE GAVE ME A NEW SONG

My next stop that week was with my voice coach—the therapist who had worked frantically with me when my voice looked like it might be coming back eighteen months before. Then, she had worked with me to focus on manufacturing the semivoice that seemed to be breaking out. Now, she was amazed that I didn't have to think about making a sound at all. I spoke as easily as I did before my primary vocal cords were ruined.

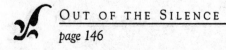

Most of you will never know how much you take your voice for granted. Imagine that in order to see something, you had to first concentrate and tell your brain, "look" and "focus." It would be exhausting, wouldn't it?

Well, that's what it was like for me to speak. I had learned to use my false cords, but I had to do it consciously, thinking about how to make the sounds as I also thought about what to say. Since my healing, the "mechanics" of speaking take care of themselves. I have never once had to "manufacture" a sound. Just like before my ailment, the voice comes out naturally.

Since there was absolutely nothing wrong with my speech, the therapist decided to try me out singing scales. As I went up and down the scales, my therapist's jaw dropped in astonishment. Then she decided to really go for it. She took me to E flat above high C, and when I hit it, she stopped playing the piano and looked at me, tears running freely down her cheeks.

"Duane," she said, astonished, "a man your age who has sung and spoken professionally loses the highs. You shouldn't be able to hit E flat above high C. You just can't *do* that."

Immediately, the Holy Spirit reminded me of Psalm 103:5, "Who satisfies your mouth with good things, / So that your youth is renewed like the eagle's."

Again, my healing was a living parable of God's truth. So many people feel that they have wasted their lives, but God does more than forgive. He can give us our youth back!

I smiled, went home, gathered up my music track tapes, and went back to my office (a space I had continued to keep after the investigative work fell through). With an incredible feeling of satisfaction and joy, I inserted the first tape into the machine. When the music first started, I felt a rush in my soul. As it led up to the part where the singer was supposed to begin, my heart practically exploded. Finally, the bar of my entrance came and I stepped back and burst forth into song. When the first piece was over, my appetite was only whetted, and I spent hours singing my favorite songs, hitting notes I hadn't hit even before I lost my voice.

*Duane Miller*

Tears streaked my cheeks as I reveled in my restoration. The long, dark night was over. Dawn was breaking. My voice was back.

I went home and sang some more songs, this time with Joylene. We held hands and cried, and my heart broke when I realized never again would we stand silent during a Christmas Eve worship service. We'd be the loudest ones there!

## TONGUES LOOSED

The rest of my days that week were spent answering the dozens of calls that came in from all over the city and the country. Since I've been in business and in the ministry in Houston for many, many years, I received calls all day long from former colleagues and acquaintances who had heard about my ordeal and the healing.

I was kept too busy and too overwhelmed even to begin thinking about my next vocational step. I was rarely given even thirty minutes to myself, and the emotions that were unleashed within me were so powerful and so profound that I'm not sure I could have kept still for longer than thirty minutes anyway.

On Friday night, the Catacombs class had a celebration party. The dinner had already been scheduled; it was part of a "Zip Code" party that was held on a regular basis to help class members who live near each other get better acquainted. While we called them Zip Code parties, a better name would be "Zip Code Buster" parties, because everybody crashed them anyway. And once word got out that I'd be coming to the next one, people came from all over.

At the party, people kept asking us to play the tape of the Sunday school class over and over. As I looked around the circle, I saw that people were mesmerized by the power of that encounter, and again, I was overwhelmed by God's foresight. There are 168 hours in every week. I taught for less than one. Had my voice been restored in any other hour, the miracle wouldn't have been recorded. It would have been just as meaningful to Joylene and me, but the literally millions of people who have since heard about it wouldn't have been able to share in its power.

Of course, at the time, I had no idea that my story would go out to millions. I was surprised, in fact, when I learned that some of the class members had invited friends and neighbors to the Zip Code party. "You've got to meet this guy," they said. "You've got to hear this tape." I became overwhelmed at the number of Catacombs and church members who were now talking to unsaved neighbors about my experience.

*God did more than restore my voice*, I thought. *He's given a new voice of evangelism to the entire church.*

Johnny Walker, a longtime member of the class, was a good example. "Electronic evangelism has always turned me off," he said. "People come, they get excited, but two weeks later, nothing has changed.

"And the healings . . . " he laughed. "Well, even as a believer, I was always a bit skeptical, watching it on television. How did I *know* they were really sick in the first place, much less healed?"

Johnny paused, looking at the group. "But because I saw this healing for myself, I knew it was genuine. There wasn't a doubt in my mind, and that gave me the confidence to talk to people I never would have talked to before."

Other heads nodded. One woman shared that she took a copy of the tape and gave it to her boss.

"Here," she told him, "you've got to listen to this. We'll talk about it later."

My heart burned as I heard these stories. Another man shared, "When I shook Duane's hand that morning, my hand tingled. It was amazing. I returned to my seat, and there was another grown man beside me, crying like a baby. I just couldn't believe the power with which the Holy Spirit visited us that day."

Another woman said, "I didn't realize how much it was hurting you, Duane, to speak to us, until I listened to the tape. It must have been awful."

Joylene grabbed my arm.

Another man added, "I think the thing that amazed me was how everybody had pretty much accepted your condition. For the first year or so, we prayed all the time, but I bet there weren't but two or three people who were still praying on the Sunday you were healed."

A woman piped in. "That's what made it so surprising. Nobody expected it. I kept thinking, 'Am I imagining this, or is his voice normal?' I leaned over to ask my husband, who looked like he had just seen a ghost, and then I realized I really *had* heard it."

All of us laughed. "I'll say," a gentlemen said. "I got some hearing aids fitted last week. I kept fiddling with the darn things when, all the sudden, Duane's voice came back. My first thought was, 'Wow, these things really work!'"

The class roared at that one.

"I wasn't surprised." Everybody's eyes turned to our dear friend Muril Wilson. Muril and her husband, Robert, were the ones who had lent us the beach house in Galveston. They had walked with us through every day of our ordeal.

"You know that first yelp on the tape?" she asked. We nodded.

"Well, that one's mine. As soon as Duane said the word 'pit,' it was as if God made it clear to me what was happening. I grabbed Robert's arm and said, 'Yes, yes, yes!'"

"I felt the same way," Larry added.

The one thread that tied together everybody's testimony, however—for this truly was a "shared healing" if ever there was one—was the power of evangelism that had taken hold of our church. Because people had witnessed a concrete miracle, they developed new courage. Because they had a new tool—a simple audio cassette—they were able to approach more people than they had ever approached before.

I remembered how, just a few days before, the realization of God's forgiveness hit me as soon as I stepped outside of Baylor Medical Center. In healing my throat, God had unleashed the tongues of thousands of others, all of whom were now eager to share the good news.

## BACK IN CLASS

Boy, what a difference a miracle makes! Joylene and I entered the Catacombs class the next Sunday feeling like royalty! A week before, I felt so low that an ant could have jumped over me. Now, you had to scrape me off the ceiling just to shake my hand!

Nobody wanted any more teaching. At the beginning of the class, somebody asked me, "So Duane, what are you going to do to top last week? Are you suddenly going to be 6-foot-4, or are you going to have hair?"

"I think I'll be 6-foot-4," I answered. "I've already had hair."

We began the class by listening to a bit of last week's tape, crying, and rejoicing all over again. And then it was time for "Duane Miller, LIVE."

I walked up on the stage and cued the sound man who immediately started the track to "Jesus, Just the Mention of Your Name." This was the song I had sung at Brenham three years before, the last song I had sung before I lost my voice. By singing this song, I felt I was picking up my ministry where I had left it. It was the final declaration of victory.

I wanted to sing it for the people who had "retrieved" me and given me the forum to continue my ministry. When I reached for the notes they were all there, like old friends who came eagerly back for the reunion. It felt wonderful having the words slide rather than grate as they left my throat. There was no pain, just plenty of unadulterated joy.

Though I'd like to think my performance experience had something to do with it, the truth is, God's miraculous healing once again stole the day. I don't think there was a dry eye in the entire class by the time I was through (Kleenex should be an official sponsor of our ministry, believe me).

Earlier in the week, I had asked Brother John if it was okay to give an invitation at the end of the class. We usually don't do that in Sunday school, but Brother John was encouraging. "Absolutely," he said. "It needs to happen."

So, after sharing some thoughts from the Word on the meaning of miracles, I gave my first invitation in three years. "God restored my voice," I said, "but even more, He wants to restore your life, your destiny, your eternal home. Won't you give Him the chance to do that this morning?"

As the people walked forward, I felt that my healing had finally come full circle. It wasn't just about me *talking* again. It was about me talking *about Jesus* again. And there was nothing I loved to do more.

## GOD'S BILLBOARDS

One of the first things a tourist notices driving through the Orlando, Florida, area is the billboards. They're all over the place. And these aren't just your average, boring billboards. Not in the land of the Magic Kingdom! These are billboards with simulated rides going up and down them, 3-D sharks moving up to devour you, and flaming lights designed to show you how much you'd just *love* to eat at a certain restaurant.

You can't miss them. Whether you speak Chinese, French, Spanish, or Arabic, you can probably figure out about 90 percent of the signs, even when zipping by at 70 mph (or crawling along at 5 mph during rush hour!).

The book of Habakkuk tells us that healings are like these billboards. God told Habakkuk that he was supposed to put his message in great big letters on a sign—in other words, a B.C. billboard—so that if someone zipped by in his chariot, he couldn't miss God's revelation.

"Write the vision and make it plain on tablets, that he may run who reads it."[3]

You see, God doesn't intend to write mysteries, where only the Sherlock Holmeses of the world can find their way into salvation. God wants the message made plain so that all who are open can understand it and receive it.

If this is the case, what better picture of a spiritual restoration can there be than to enact a physical healing? Think about it in terms of our billboard analogy. What language is a picture of a shark? What language is a photo of a happy family?

There's no answer, is there? That's because a picture is universal. In the same way, healings are healings in any language. They're God's giant billboards, telling us that supernatural power is in the air; a message that we better not miss is right around the corner.

The truth of this hit me most powerfully when I met a Vietnamese missionary who had been invited to speak at a large denominational convention. The denomination had also invited me to address the pastors and church members, which I was honored to do; but I was just as eager as anyone to hear the story of "Saul" (not his real name), a former member of the Vietcong who had become a Christian. Saul's story is the kind that makes your feet itch, it's so exciting.

After becoming disillusioned with the Vietcong, the restless Saul turned to Buddhism. If politics and war couldn't provide real peace, he thought, maybe religion could. But after becoming an adherent, Saul was turned off when he realized that there was no power in it. Next, he decided to become a Chinese magician. He was after power, and magic seemed to offer the most power available.

Saul lived fairly contentedly until some Christian missionaries came to his village. "Saul!" he was warned. "Some Christian missionaries are coming! They'll take away your respect!"

"Don't worry," he told his friend, "I'll pray them away."

Saul served 1,333 gods, and he had carefully memorized each name so that he could call upon them in times of need. Saul went to the missionaries' meeting, eager to call upon each god and send the missionaries back where they came from. His reasoning was simple: They called upon one God, whereas he had over a thousand at his disposal. How could he possibly lose?

Saul sat down at the meeting, rubbed his hands together, and then started praying. He never made it past the tenth god.

Though he tried as hard as he could to concentrate, Saul kept forgetting their names. It had been second nature for him to rattle off the list, but tonight, his mind kept wandering. At first, Saul was thrown into confusion and panic, and then a strange but welcomed peace began to seep into his spirit. Finally, when his heart was warmed sufficiently to embrace the truth, a new understanding dawned in Saul's heart.

"That's it!" he said to himself. "The gospel is more powerful than my magic."

Saul became a Christian that night, and he soon threw himself as eagerly into the faith as he had thrown himself into the world of magic. Before long, the authorities suffered through his first imprisonment.

I say *the authorities* suffered his first imprisonment because Saul's faith was so potent that he made the officials' atheistic lives miserable. Saul began preaching the gospel to his cell mates—most of whom were political prisoners—and witnessed more conversions inside prison than he had seen outside it. The authorities said, "Enough of this," and transferred Saul to a regular jail, one that held murderers, rapists, thieves, and other individuals the authorities reasoned wouldn't be so interested in Saul's message.

Not only were the inmates interested, but Saul's warden also became a Christian. Even worse, the warden took over Saul's assigned duties, such as sweeping the cell, so that Saul would have more time to evangelize the rest of the population!

Well, the authorities soon caught on, so they decided, "If we can't shut him up, we can show him to be a hypocrite."

They threw Saul into an all-female prison for prostitutes. Saul was soon surrounded by women who had made their living by seducing or accommodating men.

More than two hundred of them gave their hearts to the Lord!

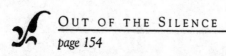

Eventually, the authorities gave up and released Saul. In all, he had spent over thirty years of his life in and out of prison as the authorities tried in vain to shut him up.

I was mesmerized by his story and humbled by the powerful way God had used him. After his talk, Joylene and I hung around the back of the room and then walked over to the elevators. You could have read the entire Pentateuch by the time these clunkers made it from the top floor to the bottom, so Joylene and I tried to wait patiently as we watched the little elevator lights crawl toward the lobby.

Saul walked up before the next elevator came down, and I took the opportunity to shake his hand and introduce myself.

"Duane Miller?" he asked, astonished. "Duane Miller?"

I shook my head "yes."

"Oh, my brother!" he said. "I can't tell you how thrilled I am to meet you. You have no idea how God has used you in Vietnam."

Since I had never *been* to Vietnam, I was intrigued, to say the least.

"We made copies of your tape—" then he stopped. "I hope you don't mind?"

"Hey, that tape is copyrighted," I responded. "When you get it, copy it, right away."

Saul laughed. "We send the tapes out to Buddhist homes. They can't understand what you're saying, of course, but when your voice changes, they always cry, always cry. Then, they ask, 'Why? How? What happened to this man?' And the worker shares Jesus with them."

He shook my hand vigorously and added, "You have no idea how many people in Vietnam have come to Christ because of you."

Of course I was humbled, overwhelmed, and awed. My faith didn't reach up to heaven and yank the healing down. My wisdom didn't figure out how to get God to move. God sovereignly decided, on His own, to overcome the natural course of events, and my throat just happened to be in the way!

*Duane Miller*

But notice how the Vietnamese, who couldn't even understand what I was saying, were moved to tears by listening to the tape of my healing. That's what I mean when I say that healings are healings in any language—God's billboard of a supernatural presence that prepares the way for the gospel.

You see, God's desire is to build an *eternal* relationship with us. Our perspective is so often temporary. We want immediate physical relief, all the while our souls and spirits crave for eternal reality.

## A NEW LIFE

So, God had given me my life back. My voice was restored, the initial euphoria was past. What else could God have in store for me?

More than I ever could have dreamed.

# chapter thirteen

## *Five Elements
of Healing
Prayer*

DUANE, WILL YOU PRAY FOR
ME?"

I had just finished preaching at a community church one Sunday morning when a woman made this request.

"I'd be delighted to pray with you," I said, and her face brightened. "But I want to tell you about a deal I made with God."

The woman's face fell into confusion.

"My deal is this: I'm going to pray that God will heal you on Tuesday."

Now she *really* looked confused. "Why would you do a thing like that?" she asked.

"Because I leave town on Monday. I want you to be healed when no one is in the room except you and God. Then, when the healing comes, no one can take the credit. You've tolerated your condition this long; surely you can handle it for another couple of days."

Because God miraculously healed me, I get requests to pray for people all the time, as if I had some kind of secret hotline to heaven that others don't. Sometimes, I wonder if people think heaven works like this: The archangel Michael looks down on earth and sees me on my knees. He rushes off to God: "Uh, God, you've got a prayer coming up from Duane Miller. Better take it; it must be very important."

Believe me, folks, it doesn't happen like that. God doesn't love me any more than He loves you. He doesn't treat my prayers any differently than He treats the prayers of people who have lived their entire lives with multiple sclerosis or cerebral palsy.

On the other hand, because of my three-year ordeal with sickness and because of my experience with personally receiving a miraculous healing, I do have a certain perspective for which God will hold me accountable to share. To that end, I'd like to discuss five elements of healing prayer; but before I do this, let me reiterate one point: The primary authority I have to share these five elements with you doesn't come because I had my voice restored. It comes from being a pastor who has studied the Word of God in season and out of season. My own healing has added "flavor" to my insight, but the "meat" of my teaching must always come from Scripture.

## 1. FIRST THINGS FIRST

The first lesson I've learned is that healing may be the engine God gives to move us forward, but the engine is pulling a little caboose called *responsibility*. This is something that I try to impart to all the people who ask me to pray for them. According to Scripture, receiving a healing is tantamount to accepting a commission: "For everyone to whom much is given, from him much will be required."[1] The NIV uses the word *demanded*. Not asked for, not requested, but *demanded*.

That's why, when people ask me to pray for them, I ask them if they are prepared to accept the responsibility that goes with it. Many seem surprised at this request. A few are offended. Some have even walked away.

I remember one Sunday in particular. A well-dressed woman came up to me and asked me to pray for her. I started to speak but felt halted by the Holy Spirit. How did I know it was the Holy Spirit? That's hard to explain, but I liken it to the way a husband just *knows* that his wife is upset, even when she insists otherwise. In our relationship with God, we can get to know Him in such a way that, though we don't hear an audible voice, we know He's speaking to us.

I believed that God had put a question in my mind, so I asked it. "How will you respond if we pray today and nothing happens?" I asked her.

A look of suspicion cast a shadow over her face. "What do you mean?" she asked.

"Well, if I pray for you, and you don't see any immediate or obvious results, how are you going to respond?"

She slowly backed up about three feet, looking at me like my head had just swiveled around on my neck, and said, "I don't think I want you to pray for me after all." She then turned and walked away.

I didn't expect to see her again, but she showed up that night for the evening service. When I finished speaking, she came forward. As she drew near, I saw that her eyes were swollen with fresh tears.

"I was so angry with you when I left here today," she told me. Her voice had been softened by repentance, and she had lost the bitter edge that cut her words earlier in the day. "But all afternoon I couldn't get away from what you said to me this morning. Finally, about four o'clock this afternoon, it dawned on me that I really had been as mad at God as I was at you."

She paused and then went on. "I want to thank you for being true to what God spoke to your heart."

*God's purpose was not so much to heal her body but to heal her soul.* She was concerned about her physical body, but God was concerned about her spiritual relationship with Him.

The same is true with you and me. God is far more concerned with my character than He is with my comfort. And yet I find that most prayers for healing have to do with physical comfort, rather than with character and right relationship with God.

If God heals me and restores my physical body, what then? How is the kingdom of God going to be benefited if that healing takes place? You see, *that's the key,* that's where the responsibility lies for those who are healed. So again, before I pray for someone's healing, I ask them first if they are ready to accept the responsibility that goes with it.

I *don't* mean that we should be reluctant when we pray. Scripture is full of verses urging us to pray for the needs of others.[2] But God never meant for healing to be a circus for the capricious amusement of His saints. On the contrary, it is serious business with serious responsibilities.

## 2. HONEST PRAYERS

In addition to *responsible* prayers, I've learned the importance of *honest* prayers. It's surprising how few people really get honest with God. When you think about it, it makes no sense. God sees all, God knows all, and God even reads our innermost thoughts in the darkest watches of the night. There isn't a single emotion, thought, or action that has entered our existence that hasn't first registered with God.

It is so futile to lie to Him, but that's what we do, isn't it? My heart breaks over the dishonesty and hypocrisy in the church. People are afraid to say to God, "I hurt and I don't like this," or "I don't understand what's going on and I'm afraid!"

You should have heard some of my prayers. I never lost my foundational belief in the sovereignty of God, but I also wasn't afraid to let God know what I was thinking: "God, I'm angry. This makes no sense to me. You've called me to preach, but now it's like you've sent me out to pasture—and I'm not even fifty years old. Where are you? Aren't you paying attention?"

I was as honest with God as I could be, and obviously, that didn't stop God from healing me!

I wonder sometimes if, deep down, we really don't believe God cares enough about us to deal with the heart issues that cut us so deeply. We'll rush to pray about a broken leg, but feel guilty about praying for a broken heart. Instead of saying to

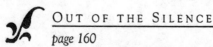

God, "I'm hurt and I'm scared and I need your help," we walk around with smiles on our faces, telling people we're just fine and we know God's going to get us through.

David certainly didn't try to hide his fear and weakness from God. Even a quick glance at the Psalms is enough to show us how deeply honest David was with God—and David was a man God said was "after my own heart." David's honesty didn't keep him from God; on the contrary, it drew him to God, and honesty will do the same for us.

## 3. PERSPECTIVE

In the midst of our honesty, however, we must leave room for *God's perspective*, which far exceeds our own. We live life looking through a tiny hole, like a young boy peeking through the fence, trying to get a glimpse of a major league baseball game. God's view, however, is more akin to one provided by the Goodyear blimp. He sees it all. There are no angles hidden from his view, no set of bleachers that He could possibly miss. So though we need to be honest, we also need to leave room for God's superior understanding.

My father was a drill sergeant in World War II. Whoever trained him taught him well, because it was a skill he never lost. He was very strict, and even today, I can feel his webbed belt convincing me that whatever offense I had committed wasn't really worth the price I was paying.

Today, I see kids throw food off their plates, saying, "I won't eat this." You wouldn't do that with my dad. If you did, you'd only do it once.

Just before I reached the exalted state of adolescence, I decided to be smart and try a slightly less direct approach to refusing food. My mother placed a large platter of liver on the table, and I said, choosing each word carefully, "I don't want to eat that."

Notice I didn't say I *won't* eat that; I said I didn't *want* to eat that. Surely my dad couldn't punish me for expressing an opinion, right?

Well, he didn't punish me, but he didn't give in, either. "You don't want to eat that?" he asked me, his eyebrows raised.

"No," I said.

"Then just sit there until you do," he responded.

I did.

During those years, especially when the leather of my dad's belt introduced itself to the bare skin of my backside, I sometimes wondered if my dad really loved me. Now, I have absolutely no doubt. Being a father myself, I realize he wanted to raise me the best way he knew how. I was just too young to see it. While I once thought he was sent to earth to destroy my "fun," I now realize he was commissioned by God to raise a healthy, God-fearing boy who would achieve his full God-given potential.

This perspective helped me to better understand what was going on during my three-year ordeal with my throat. By my reckoning, my malady went on about two years, eleven months, and three weeks longer than necessary. By God's timing, it was just right.

Yet honestly, I *did* begin to question God's love. How *could* He love me, I thought, when He allows me to suffer like this? I tried to remind myself: *Remember how you felt when your father disciplined you? You were certain he didn't love you, yet now you have no doubt. The same will be true of your feelings toward God. Just wait it out, and you'll see.*

My feelings didn't automatically change, but my perspective did. Looking back, I can see God's loving care every second of the way. There wasn't a blink of an eye that passed without God's love covering it.

And yet I don't believe that God was upset with me when I was honest with Him about how unhappy I was. He knew my perspective was limited. As a little boy looking through the big-league fence, I saw one event at a time. As a God of eternity, He saw my healing in His overall plan.

God has big shoulders. My tears didn't speed up the arrival of my healing, but they didn't slow it down either. My honest prayers didn't alienate me from God, nor did they make Him love me more; He already loves me perfectly.

What they did do, however, was to help me let go of all those negative feelings that were eating me inside. If we can't do that with God, who else is there? Denial doesn't help anyone. Getting honest with God helps everyone.

Getting the proper perspective means remembering that God doesn't cause any problems. He allows them, certainly, but He doesn't cause them. In fact, it was out of mercy that God didn't immediately answer my most angry prayers. The only suitable answer to them would have been a lightning bolt!

I don't pray with "thees" and "thous" anymore. I don't try to be "spiritual." God speaks Swahili, Mandarin Chinese, Arabic, you name it. I'm sure He can also handle good old colloquial English. I'll save the "spiritual" stuff for the professional religious folks. For me, I'll be content with honesty.

That's the language God really speaks.

## 4. UNDERSTANDING THE LESSON

One Sunday morning, as I wrapped up a sermon at a Presbyterian church, I yearned to give an invitation, but as is typical with most Presbyterian buildings, there was no place to invite people to come forward. (Talk about tying a Baptist preacher's hands behind his back!) One of a preacher's secret skills is learning to talk while thinking something else through, but on this occasion I ran out of sermon before I ran into inspiration, so I simply said, "Whatever pit you're in, God is concerned. Please stand for prayer."

And then the battle began. God's unmistakable "still small voice" broke into my silence and I sensed Him saying, *Someone here has arthritis in the left knee. It is so bad they are unable to walk. Call them out.*

A Baptist pastor's second secret skill is learning to argue with God while ostensibly praying to Him!

*But, Lord,* I argued. *This is a Presbyterian church (as if He didn't know). They don't understand that sort of thing.*

*Do it.*

*But Lord,* I argued once again. *This type of thing doesn't happen to me. And if this is gonna start to happen, does it really have to be in a Presbyterian church?*

God's spiritual pressure beamed in on me like a laser. I wasn't going to be able to argue my way out of this one anymore than Jonah was able to argue his way out of Nineveh. I swallowed hard, tried not to notice the sweat running in little trickles down my back, and said, "Okay folks, I'm going to do something that you may not understand. I know that what I'm about to do is not according to your tradition, but I need to be true to what I believe God is saying to me."

I took a deep breath. I felt like a young kid jumping off the high dive for the first time. "I sense the Spirit of God speaking to my heart, telling me that someone here has arthritis so badly in the left knee that it is impossible to stand up, even though you'd like to. Is anybody here like that, or is it the pizza I ate last night?"

Inside my soul, the consistency of my fortitude was somewhere between Jell-O and oatmeal. I was fully aware that what I was doing was in direct challenge to their doctrine, tradition, and personal experience. If I was wrong, I could cost the young pastor his pulpit for inviting me, and I didn't take that lightly. On the other hand, the spiritual pressure was so intense that I realized I could not *not* do it.

My heart beat so hard I thought it was bruising the inside of my chest. The longest five seconds of my life passed until a little woman in her late sixties, about three or four rows from the front, waved her hand at me.

My fear vanished. God wouldn't be this specific—arthritis in the left knee—if He wasn't about to do something about it. And this woman's condition fit the description perfectly. The arthritis in her left knee had swollen the joint to literally grotesque proportions. That's why she waved her hand instead of standing. Standing was a physical impossibility.

Enter God, stage left.

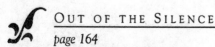

OUT OF THE SILENCE

"God wouldn't tell me this if He didn't intend to follow through and heal you," I said. "Now, I'm going to do something that's really going to blow you away because it's going to violate anything you've ever known—" I wanted these people to be prepared. My job wasn't to be the ringmaster or master magician, but an explainer of God's Word, so I wanted to take the congregation through this slowly.

"I believe that if you will grab the pew in front of you," I was talking directly to the woman now, "that's it, just grab onto the pew in front of you . . . Okay, now, try to stand to your feet. God wants to heal you."

This dear woman grabbed the pew with decades-weathered hands and began to struggle to pull herself upright. As she did so, a collective gasp from the people around her shot through the air. Their mouths dropped open and some of their faces turned white as they watched her knee shrink to its normal size, right in front of their eyes!

Years melted away as I saw the smile of a child on Christmas morning come across the face of that woman. She stepped out into the aisle, flexed her knee, and began moving around in a way she hadn't done for years.

The congregation was murmuring and crying, some were audibly gasping. The woman's daughter ran up from the back, let out a shriek, and embraced her mother. Both woman started weeping. They hugged and sobbed, and I noted with mixed irony and glee that this church probably wouldn't remember a word I had said, but they would never forget this day.

After the daughter had regained composure, she faced the church and said, "You all know my mother and how bad her arthritis has been. There have been days lately when I would have to go over to her house in the morning and literally help her get out of bed because her knee was so stiff she couldn't move. And look at her now!"

The congregation erupted into spontaneous applause. People began weeping (the young pastor—a godly and promising man—was one of them), members hugged each other, and I heaved a huge sigh of relief.

I then concluded the service by bringing back my scar tissue analogy, relating it to this woman's knee. Just as God can remove our ugly diseases, things we thought we simply had to learn to live with, so He will forgive our ugly sins. This healing isn't about a sideshow, I said, it's about God offering forgiveness, using this woman's knee as an example.

"If that's coming through, if that's speaking to your heart this morning, I want you to stand."

Dozens of people did so, and the kingdom of God was increased.

I relate this to illustrate the fourth element in healing prayer: we need to ask God what He wants us to learn and do in our situation, because God has a specific *purpose* for every single thing He does. The purpose here was to demonstrate His power in a nonthreatening way to people who had never seen that sort of thing before. I'm sure there were many other people there that day with heart problems, similar arthritic problems, and the like, but God was able to make His point by showcasing one, nonthreatening healing.

In doing this, God created a community of people who now *know* what God can do because they've witnessed His power. And there are new believers who were willing to consider the message of forgiveness because they personally witnessed something for which there was no rational explanation.

Now, I'd like to tell you that everywhere I go, that same sort of miraculous thing happens, but it doesn't. If a church invites me, hoping to get a bargain discount on their congregation's medical bills, they're as likely as not to be disappointed. Healing isn't something I can turn on and off at will. It comes when God wills, when He has a particular point to get across to a particular congregation.

We need to remember that the primary purpose of miraculous healing isn't to make us feel good. If people want me to pray for them, and I ask them why, and they say, "Because I just want to feel better," I'm tempted to say, "If all you want is to feel better, then I'm going to pray that you'll die. You'll feel fine, then. The purpose of healing is not to feel better, it's to point people to the cross."

I would be remiss if I let the healings occur without tying them into the corresponding message and helping the congregation learn what the purpose of each particular miracle is. That's my role as the teacher.

## 5. BE OPEN!

The final element of healing prayer is simply a *willingness* to let it happen. If we pray honestly, with a willingness to accept the responsibility, keeping the right perspective and seeking the lesson God wants to teach us, then the rest is up to God. If somebody asked me to give a short answer to the question, "How should I pray?" I'd say, "Pray honestly, and pray to be used of God *right where you are*, problems and all." God may use you by healing you, or He may use you in the midst of your illness—either way, He wants to use you. It's His choice how He does that.

What does this mean? It may mean going to the hospital to have surgery and being healed there so that you can share Jesus with the person in the next bed. It may mean accepting a miracle on the spot. We cannot dictate to God how He heals. If He chooses to heal the way He healed the woman with the arthritic knee, He undoubtedly has a reason behind it. If He chooses to heal through surgery, He also has a reason (it just may be the last opportunity that the attending physician has to hear the gospel of Christ). Maybe a relative needs to see us bear our difficulties with the right spirit so that he or she can see that our faith is real.

Either way, we need to be open to being used of God, because that's what we are—tools in the Master Craftsman's hands. We should strive to be open to instant healing, open to surgery, and open to months of drawn-out therapy. Everything in the kingdom revolves around being used of God for His purposes and for His glory, and that can only be done when it's done *His way.*

Many people feel that unless a healing happens in a manner similar to what happened to me it isn't really a "miracle." I emphatically disagree with that. You see, my family has witnessed more than one miracle of healing. The one I'm going to tell you about in the next chapter happened in a much different manner than the way in which my voice was restored, but it's still a startling example of God's healing touch. It wasn't what we typically think of as "supernatural," instantaneous, or miraculous. If you talk to my daughter Jodi, however, you'll realize the miracle performed in her life was every bit as precious as the one God performed in mine.

# chapter fourteen

# Quiet Miracles and the Role of Faith

OUR DAUGHTER JODI IS A VERY easy person to like. There are some people that you like (or tolerate) because you have to—maybe you try to get along with them because they're members of your church, they're your coworkers, or they're related to you in some way—and then there are those people who are almost impossible not to like. Their personalities are inviting, they lack the hard edges that cause offense, and they have something interesting to say.

Jodi is like that. Her friendships run deep, and her warm manner is inviting to strangers as well. She's always been a good student and never gotten into any "serious trouble." God has blessed her with some close girlfriends, and growing up, she also had her share of boyfriends.

You'd think that with such a personality she would have a fairly positive view of herself, but in today's world, that's not necessarily true.

In Jodi's senior year of high school in 1989, while our family was still tucked away in Brenham, Jodi became obsessed with reaching a certain weight. She had a very attractive figure and getting dates was never a problem, but Jodi still felt compelled to lose another ten pounds.

Perhaps we should have noticed. Perhaps we should have been suspicious when Jodi said, "No thanks, Mom, I'll grab a bite to eat later." But it never occurred to us that Jodi had no intention of "grabbing a bite to eat later." And many times, we did see her eat a healthy meal.

What we didn't see were her trips to the bathroom afterwards, where she would force herself to throw up.

The long and tentacled arms of bulimia had reached into our house. Jodi struggled bravely on her own for several months until one afternoon when she looked particularly weak, and her best friend and boyfriend sat her down, learned the truth, and said, "If you don't tell your mom, we will."

"Just let me lose another eight pounds," Jodi insisted. "Then I'll quit."

"No." Her friends, thank God, were forceful. "You tell her tonight, or we tell her tonight. Those are your only options."

That afternoon, Joylene came home and saw a tired and wan Jodi sitting on the couch waiting for her.

"What is it, honey?" Joylene asked.

Jodi started crying. Joylene rushed over to hold her.

"Mom, I have to tell you something," Jodi began, her voice broken by tears. "Dathan and Julie said I have to tell you or they will."

"Tell me what?"

"I'm bulimic. I'm making myself throw up, and I'm taking laxatives."

Joylene held her youngest daughter as tightly as she could, whispering affirmations of love, mixing her tears with Jodi's. It was then that she remembered Jodi's questions earlier in the week.

"Do I look pale to you, Mom? Do I look thin?"

At the time, Joylene was simply confused by Jodi's questions. She had never been able to put them together, so she had simply answered, "Honey, you look great." Now, finally, she

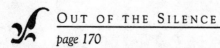

understood. Her little girl, the one who would always have a cherished place in her heart, was rebelling against her own body for some unknown reason.

I was out of town, so Joylene immediately took Jodi to a counseling center, and there she discovered to her horror why a can of Drano was inexplicably left beside the sink.

"I thought I had eaten too much," Jodi confessed, "and I knew that Drano cleaned pipes, so I thought, maybe, that it could clean me out as well."

Now, Jodi's not dumb. She was an excellent student. But desperation has a way of twisting even an intelligent person's logic and understanding. Jodi's situation had degenerated to such a point that she was no longer thinking clearly. Thank God, she had never acted on this false logic, but it was a terrifying experience for Joylene to put that can of Drano away, thinking "what if?"

I was attending a relative's funeral when Jodi first told Joylene. When I returned home, tired and somber, I was also completely unprepared for the scene I was about to walk into.

Joylene hadn't been able to get a hold of me, so she was doing her best to get Jodi through the initial trauma until my homecoming. Just hours before my plane landed, however, Jodi had been left alone for just fifteen minutes, and during that time she panicked and made herself throw up. She told Joylene immediately, and the revelation was enough to break them both. Bulimia and anorexia are as terrifying as they are mystifying, and Joylene and Jodi were completely exhausted by the time I arrived home.

As soon as I stepped inside the door, I heard a loud cry, "Daadddy!" The cry was full of desperation, yet tinged with relief that I had finally made it home.

"What is it?" I asked. I saw both Jodi and Joylene crying uncontrollably, and it took me several minutes finally to understand why these two precious women were weeping.

As a father, my anger can rise at the mere thought of somebody attempting any harm against either of my daughters. I would willingly and gladly give my life for them. In addition to praying for them, I had spent considerable amounts of time ruminating on ways to protect them. I grilled their boyfriends. I made sure we knew they'd be going to safe places. I worked hard to put them in good schools. In short, I did my best to protect them against every known threat.

But the disease of bulimia is a predator that strikes from within. It was an enemy against which I felt completely powerless.

I immediately got on the phone and called a friend of mine who works with a Christian counseling organization called Rapha.

"Al," I asked in desperation, "what do I do?"

Here I was, a pastor, supposedly the one with all the answers, but this tragedy had struck too close to home.

Al asked some very specific questions, then said, "Don't worry, don't panic, she won't die, and she isn't suicidal, but *get her to me* tomorrow morning. Understand? I want to see her tomorrow at ten o'clock. No excuses."

"She'll be there," I promised.

"And one other thing. Don't leave her alone. Somebody should always be by her side, even if she's in the bathroom."

"Done," I said.

The next morning we drove from Brenham to Houston and had Jodi admitted to the hospital where Rapha had a special unit. It was a sobering experience, believe me. We went through locked doors, then had to pass through a metal detector to get to the elevator. An attendant had to use one key to get on the elevator and another key to get off. Next, we went through an additional set of locked doors to get to the actual unit.

The reason for all this security is that the counseling center works with some very troubled people. Some have drug addictions, some are alcoholics, others are struggling with bulimia, and still others are suicidal. Rapha's basic premise, however, is that whatever the activity, it is only the symptom, not the disease. The center was determined to treat the disease, and thereby disengage the symptom.

Jodi began receiving very specific Christian instruction from the Scriptures regarding her identity in Christ. Though her actions had caused her soul to begin to unravel, these dedicated and well-trained believers worked carefully and meticulously to put her back together.

Part of that process involved family counseling. It was there that I realized how my hectic lifestyle as a businessman and then pastor had affected my daughters in their formative years. I'm embarrassed to admit this (if you're looking for a hero with no skeletons in his closet, I'm sorry to disappoint you), but Jodi's desperation forced me to own up to some very painful neglect. I had been so busy making a living and doing "good things" at the church, helping other people to solve their problems, that I often had no time for my own family.

"Daddy," Jodi admitted, "you're just not there for us. You're always there for everybody else, but not for us."

I couldn't argue with her. In fact, when I took an honest look back, I realized that the more successful I became, the less I was at home. I was reminded of when my business interests took off and our family suddenly found ourselves in the enclave of the wealthy. I worked full-time in the insurance business, bought an oil company "on the side," and served on the staff of a church.

For a time, my daughters had everything they could ever want—except their dad.

On one occasion, Joylene heard our daughters complaining about it. "We haven't seen Daddy in over a week," Lisa said. "I liked it better when we didn't have a lot of money."

I deeply regret that I wounded my children in these years, and with all my heart I wish I could go back, but of course, I can't. I can only trust God to bring the healing that is necessary.

Down in my gut, I knew Jodi's confession was 100 percent accurate. I had to face my own failings as a father. I had to change. I had to find ways to be there for Jodi in the future.

Even though Jodi grew up hearing godly teaching, and even though she had accepted Jesus Christ as her Savior and Lord, it wasn't until that intense thirty-day period that the truth of who she was in Christ got down inside her spirit and set her free.

Jodi left Rapha knowing that the Word of God could be trusted, that God's love was absolute and certain, and that there was nothing that would come into her life that God would not first permit. From the day she left Rapha, Jodi accomplished something that is extremely rare for bulimia patients: She has never had even the slightest relapse.

People unfamiliar with this malady may not realize how much of a miracle this is. Jodi was not only bulimic, she was also diagnosed as borderline anorexic. Either one of these can be extremely difficult to cure, and many women die annually from these behaviors. For Jodi to break free from both of them is truly a work of God. Food addictions are even more difficult to break than drug or sexual addictions because the stimulus is always right there. A drug addict can avoid drugs, but a bulimic can't get away from food.

Yet God literally put Jodi back together in such a way that she developed a healthy attitude toward food and her own body. Her healing was every bit as much a miracle as mine, even though some people might disqualify it from being a miracle because it didn't happen "instantaneously."

But you know what? Her problems were created by a process, and a process was the most effective way in which she could be healed. Part of that healing meant confronting me about my own failings as a father. If God had just "zapped" her well, an important element in our family's healing would have been missing, one that I particularly treasure. Even though our daughters no longer live at home, I have a better relationship with them today than ever before.

In this instance, I firmly believe that God used Scripture, daily counseling, and family discussion to enact a "long-term miracle." No matter how God chooses to heal—whether instantaneously or through a process—the healing is from Him, and we need to stand back and give Him all the glory.

## GOD'S SOVEREIGNTY AND OUR RESPONSE

Our acceptance of these "quiet miracles" is so important because they point us back to the sovereignty of God. Remember, healing is hidden in God's hands, not in ours. This is something I'm reminded of every time I look back at the circumstances of my own healing and review how God "set me up" for the miracle.

First of all, I shouldn't have been teaching that class in 1993. Before I was given charge of the class, another teacher had compelling personal circumstances that forced him to leave his teaching post prior to the end of his commitment. Anybody associated with Southern Baptist structure realizes that we take these teaching commitments seriously, so I really shouldn't have been in front of that class at all.

Second, the class asked me to teach in spite of the fact that I could hardly speak and had badly managed a retreat just a few months prior. Sure, I had learned greater mastery of my "false cords," but as you'll hear from the recording that accompanies this book, the resulting voice was enough to try anybody's patience.

Third, as a pastor, it still amazes me that the church leadership cautiously agreed to let me speak for even an "interim" period. Keep in mind, this wasn't just any church, but one of the largest churches in the country, with a Sunday school class that more than doubled the average size of a United States congregation.

Fourth, I almost chuckle now when I hear how they were stymied in their efforts to find a replacement long after my "interim" period was finished. A church with more than twenty thousand members really shouldn't have a difficult time finding a Sunday school teacher—unless perhaps the God of the universe was standing in the way.

Fifth, I did not choose the material I taught from that morning. It was not some late-night stroke of inspiration by which I picked Psalm 68 and Psalm 103. The passage I was scheduled to speak on was taken from the Southern Baptist Convention Bible Book Series. This series is scheduled seven years in advance, so this lesson went on the calendar back in 1986. And trust me on this one—the person who wrote the lesson did not have a parentheses (INSERT HEALING HERE) to go along with the message.

Sixth, according to the schedule, I shouldn't have been teaching that particular lesson on that Sunday. It was scheduled to be taught two weeks prior, but because of a missions conference, we swapped it with another lesson. Keep in mind that if I had taught this lesson two weeks earlier, I wouldn't have faced the bottom of my pit yet. It wasn't until two days earlier—January 15—that I finally reached the floor.

God is like the consummate grandmaster chess champion, willing to sacrifice a pawn or two of inconvenience for us to be checkmated at precisely the right moment in our lives. I don't know that I could have lived another day with such futility. On the other hand, just three days earlier, I was coping all right. The window of my pit was amazingly narrow, but to God, it must have appeared as wide as the Grand Canyon, because His river of healing certainly came rushing through!

Seventh, in spite of an Assemblies of God background, I was attending and teaching Sunday school in a Southern Baptist church, which gave my healing more credibility in the eyes of the non-Pentecostals and noncharismatics. I don't mean to offend anyone by pointing that out, but we all know it's true. Now, I didn't begin pastoring in a Southern Baptist church for that reason, but in God's hand, that's how it all worked out.

Finally, because we wanted to include classmates who were occasionally out of town on business or pleasure, our classes were taped. Many, many sermons are taped across the nation on any given Sunday morning, but how many Sunday school classes are actually taped? An incredibly small percentage. The dynamics of our class, however, were such that the taping was done, which meant that the miraculous return of my voice was recorded for everyone to hear.

Does all this stuff take your breath away like it does mine? God is sovereign. He not only cares about our circumstances, He orders them. I am *not* saying that God creates all circumstances (especially the negative ones), but He does allow them—and He certainly works through them. God's sovereignty does not exist in a vacuum. God works His plans and purpose through people who have a free and often stubborn will.

God did not make us robots without minds of our own. But none of our choices—right or wrong—throw God's plans off by one millimeter. Our disobedience or foolishness does not send Him crashing down from His throne. Our obedience does not restore His crown. God knows what He is doing, and He will do it—either through us or in spite of us.

It's humbling but true: God will work where we allow Him to work. Where we won't allow Him to work, He'll accomplish His purposes anyway, though He'll do so without our help.

## A TALE OF TWO THEOLOGIES

Christians have debated the sovereignty of God and the free will of man for centuries, and there are two extreme positions that have been developed, written about, and argued. The first position is that absolutely everything is preordained. You and I have nothing to do with anything. We've either been chosen to be saved or we haven't, and there's nothing we can do about it. That's the doctrine of election taken to its extreme.

The opposing doctrine—the doctrine of free will—has also been taken to its extreme, and it argues that virtually *everything* is dependent upon me. If I have enough faith, if I act right, if I perform well, if I say the right words and develop the right disposition, then I can curry God's favor and manipulate Him into jumping through my carefully contrived hoops.

I believe that neither of these teachings, taken to an extreme, is true. Both the Old Testament and the New call us to be "temperate."[1] That means, in part, that we should be balanced in all things, including the balance between God's sovereignty and man's free will.

I realize that, again, this makes me sound like a man without a theological country, but I have to be honest about what Scripture clearly teaches, even as it has been revealed in my own circumstances. God didn't attack my throat and assault my voice because I was disobedient—I just don't believe that—and He didn't restore my voice because I had learned to adopt heroic levels of faith. God did what He did because in His wisdom He determined that was the best thing to do, and I simply got to come along for the ride.

## THE ROLE OF FAITH

Much has also been written and said about the role of faith in healing. There are many who teach (especially, it seems, on television) that if we can somehow muster up enough faith, God Himself will perform for us. Now, the Bible tells us that "without faith it is impossible to please [God]."[2] I believe that with all my heart. But the Bible also tells us that faith is a *gift*.[3] How is it, then, that God is going to give you more faith than He gives me, and then hold me responsible because I don't have enough? That would be like a father who gives one child five dollars for her allowance and another child three dollars, and then chastises the one who received three because she can't afford to buy her own ticket to the movies.

God just wouldn't do that.

Remember, we are playing in God's ballpark, and He sets the rules. As I understand Scripture, I am His servant, He is not mine. That's why I object to the "faith message" when it implies or even states directly that God can be manipulated by my activity. I've seen how this teaching has wounded so many precious souls.

When people think their potential healing will be based on faith, and the healing doesn't come, their natural reaction is to think, "What did I do wrong?" "Didn't I have enough faith?" "Did I allow doubt to creep in?"

There wasn't a millimeter's difference in my faith before and after my healing. If faith is defined as belief that God would heal me, my faith had actually *declined* by the time God restored my voice. Why, then, was I healed? Not because of my faith, but because God is sovereign, and that means things will happen in His way, on His timetable, and according to His purpose.

Believe me—I of all people know how frustrating and absolutely irritating this timetable can feel. During the beginning of my ordeal, I poured out prayers for healing more often than a leaky faucet lets go of a drip. If God had healed me back then, there's no denying that Joylene and I would have been spared much pain and anguish. But my testimony would have lacked the power it has today. When I think of the people who have been inspired by this miracle, and those precious new believers who have come to know the glories and joys of eternal life because they saw God's offer of forgiveness in a new light, I count my suffering as minuscule compared to how God has used it to build up His kingdom.

The way I look at it, many of these "faith teachers" have it backwards. *Real* faith isn't exercised when everything is going smoothly, when I have plenty of money and excellent health and a job I love and nothing or no one is causing me any real problems. Real faith blossoms and is tested when things just don't make sense; when the electricity is about to be shut off and I don't know where the money is going to come from to pay the bill; when I'm praying and nothing changes; when I'm looking for a job but no one is interested in my skills; when my spouse wants a divorce or the kids reject everything I've ever taught them and go off into illegal or immoral lifestyles. When

I can still trust and praise God in the midst of all that, I have truly laid hold of faith.

In other words, affluence, good health, and smooth waters aren't necessarily the hallmarks of someone who has laid hold of faith. It may be that God just knows their faith is too weak to be tested! Instead, we may have to look for faith in the lives of people who feel like Job is a close relative.

I can't say it enough: The incredible, miraculous healing that I received on Sunday, January 17, 1993, was not because of my great faith. It was rather because of the One in whom I had placed that faith, the sovereign God of the universe, the One who, in His mercy and according to *His* purposes, reached down and touched me—in that time, in that place, and for His glory.

## THE ROLE OF PRAYER

Well, what does that say about the role of prayer?

When my voice first left me, people all over the world began praying for me. I don't know of any major ministry or minor church that didn't have me on some sort of prayer list. My mother practically made it her full-time occupation to find new prayer chains to put me on.

And yet, in the season of all those prayers, I was never healed.

By the time my healing came, most everyone had stopped praying for my healing. We had resigned ourselves to learning to live with life as it was, not as we wanted it to be. This was a somewhat bitter resignation, but I felt it was essential for my emotional health. "Hope deferred makes the heart sick,"[4] and mine was beginning to be seriously ill.

So the question that inevitably arises is this: Do I believe I was healed as a direct result of prayer? The answer might shock some of you, so hang with me.

It's yes and no.

We are commanded in Scripture to pray for the sick.[5] But none of this is alerting God to anything He doesn't already

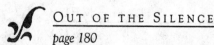

know. Nothing surprises God, nothing is news to God, so in this sense, prayer does no good. I believe God would have healed me even if the prayers offered on my behalf had never been uttered.

Now, before you close the book in disgust, let me qualify what I'm saying. Do I then believe that we should stop praying? Absolutely not. Prayer didn't tell God anything He didn't already know—that I needed and wanted healing—but it did a tremendous amount of good for me and for those who were praying. A lot of the things that came together did so, I believe, because people were praying. In fact, I would even say that those prayers were part of God's plan from the beginning.

But none of that changes the fact that *God healed me not because we had prayed long enough or hard enough or with enough faith, but because He wanted people to be drawn to Him and to give Him all the glory.* I have no doubt that there are Christians who have prayed longer, harder, and with more "faith" than we ever did, but who have yet to be healed. On the other hand, I'm sure there are people who prayed with less fervency than we did who received their healing much sooner.

I don't want to cast doubt on prayer—that's *not* my purpose here. But I do want to cast doubt on the teaching that misleads Christians into believing that, if they're healed, they "earned" their healing by their faith, and if they're not healed, it's because they failed to manufacture sufficient faith.

When I hear that teaching, I immediately think of Job's counselors, probing and prying to find out why Job was suffering as he was. Well, I've been a Job. I've had my world taken away from me, in ways few people could understand. I know what it feels like, and that's why I have a passion to remind other Christians that the entire issue of faith and prayer only makes sense within the overall umbrella of the sovereignty of God.

You see, God has a purpose behind every miracle. I firmly believe that. But what many Christians don't realize is that God also has a purpose behind every storm. We'll talk in length about this in the next chapter, as I believe it may be the most important message in this book.

# chapter fifteen

# I AM
# *in the Midst*
# *of the Storm*

IN ORDER TO UNDERSTAND THE
PURPOSE OF miracles, we need to
understand that storms have a purpose as
well. God allowing a storm to crash into our lives
can be every bit as much evidence of His love as
when He unleashes a powerful miracle of healing.
This may be the most difficult truth for Christians
to understand and accept, but I believe it is crucial for the church to learn as we approach the
next century.

God is not capricious. Everything He does is done with purpose. Storms often "set us up" to receive and perceive the
miraculous intervention of the Father. Think about it—if we're
never in danger, we don't need a Savior, do we? And if we're
never in a bind, how can we ever need a miracle?

If you are to understand my story, if you want to share my
exultant joy, you must have a grasp of the storm, as well as a
grasp of its purpose. The darker the backdrop in a painting, the
brighter the subject will appear when placed on the canvas. So
it is with our lives. It is against the backdrop of the dark storms
that the Father reveals the brilliance of His grace and glory.

That's why I've been very honest with you in sharing the
struggles I experienced during my three-year desert of silence. I

haven't pretended that there weren't any tears, doubts, anger, or frustration. You wouldn't have been able to understand my joy if you hadn't first understood my pain.

But what is true for me is true for all of us. I'm not the only one who has faced a tremendous storm. All of us, to varying degrees, find ourselves in different seasons of struggle, each one of which requires a "little miracle" for us to be delivered safely on the other side.

The fourteenth chapter of Matthew's gospel contains principles that have become cornerstones of my life and my ministry. In order for my miracle to make sense, and in order for you to gain an understanding of your own need for miracles, I believe it's crucial for us to discuss those principles here.

## SENT OUT INTO THE STORM

A friend of ours sometimes surprises his wife after church by saying, "Oh, by the way, honey, I invited a new family to our house for lunch after church. I hope you don't mind?"

"How many kids do they have?"

"Eight." He watches his wife's face fall before asking, "Is that a problem?"

Adding ten people to an impromptu lunch is enough to raise the pulse of any wife, but imagine having your Lord say to you, "Let's see what we can cook up for fifteen thousand people."

Five thousand hungry men, five thousand hungry women, and probably at least five thousand hungry children, for a total of about fifteen thousand people. And Jesus instructed the disciples to satisfy every growling stomach with a little boy's lunch. (The real miracle, some say, was that a boy still had his lunch at that hour!)

Now imagine being one of the disciples. Imagine that, in spite of your doubts, you went ahead and did it. And then, you saw the miracle unfold. Afterwards, you lift your fingers in front of you, amazed that it was your hands that handed out the food and your hands that gathered in all the leftovers. You didn't

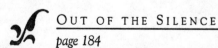

OUT OF THE SILENCE

*page 184*

notice anything going on, but somehow, out of those ordinary hands, a tremendous miracle was wrought. You don't know whether to laugh, cry, sing, or shout, but before you even have time to contemplate it, you're being instructed to get into a boat: "*Immediately* Jesus *made* His disciples get into the boat and go before Him to the other side, while He sent the multitudes away" (emphasis added).[1]

Please notice that, chronologically, this happened *immediately* following this miraculous event. There is no time lag here. As soon as the multitudes had been fed, the disciples followed Jesus down the hill to the lake, where Jesus *made* them get into the boat.

Do you understand that the disciples didn't want to get into that boat, and that in all probability, they argued with Jesus about getting into that boat?

Can't you just hear it? Jesus says to them, "Guys, I'm going to dismiss the crowds now and then go on up the hill to pray. You get in the boat and go on over to the other side and wait for me. I'll join you later."

"Oh no, Master," they reply, casting glances over their shoulders at the darkening sky. "We'll just wait here for You."

"No," Jesus says. "I want you to get in the boat and go on ahead of Me."

Again they argue. "We'd rather wait right here, Jesus, and then we can all go across together."

"You're not listening," Jesus replies, His voice becoming more forceful. "Get in the boat *now* and go."

Finally they gave in, but why do you suppose they offered so much resistance in the first place? I'll tell you why. The majority of those guys were fishermen. So isn't it likely that, when they came down off that hill with the multitudes and looked out across the lake, they saw storm clouds in the distance? Experienced fishermen are not going to want to get in a boat and go out on a lake with a storm moving in! They wanted to stay on the shore with the One who had just fed the multitudes with one little boy's lunch. Isn't that what you or I would want to do?

But Jesus insisted, and so at last they obeyed. Is it likely that Jesus was unaware of that approaching storm? Of course not. Even if He hadn't noticed it—which He undoubtedly did—the disciples would have been quick to point it out to Him. So then, what does that say to us? It says that there was a purpose for that storm and our Lord wanted His disciples to be right smack-dab in the middle of it!

How many times have we all heard the fallacy that, if we're in the midst of a storm, we must somehow be out of God's will? Obviously that was not the case with the disciples. They were commanded to go into the storm *against their will*, and if they had continued to refuse, they would have been out of *God's will*.

We need to understand this very basic principle: We can be in the midst of the greatest storm of our lives and still be right in the center of God's will! You see, the storms of life are inevitable. No one lives a storm-free life. In fact, someone once said that there are three stages in our lives: We are either entering a storm, enduring a storm, or emerging from a storm, in which case we're preparing to enter another one. (How's that for good news?)

## DISCOVERING OUR SOURCE

The next point to notice here is that these disciples weren't just fishermen, they were able-bodied seamen. They'd been in storms before—lots of them! But this was no ordinary storm. And this "lake" or "sea" they were on was no ordinary little fishing pond. A later verse paints a graphic picture: "But the boat was now in the middle of the sea, tossed by the waves, for the wind was *contrary*" (emphasis added).[2]

The word *contrary* here means more than just a head wind. Experienced sailors aren't particularly concerned about head winds. Boats can be tacked into head winds, and port can be reached without difficulty. "Contrary" here suggests that the

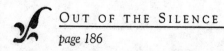

wind was their adversary. Picture the wind coming from the north. About the time the rigging is set to catch the wind, it changes and is now from the southeast. All the rigging has to be knocked down and changed to catch the wind from the southeast and, about the time it's set, the wind changes to north-northwest. The wind was against them. No matter how they set their sails, the winds would just change and come against them again. It was the first time in their long fishing career that these seamen could not get their boat safely to shore. It was, in fact, the first time they realized that all their training and all their skills and all their experience just weren't enough to get them out of this storm.

Ever been there? If you haven't, you will be! Because it's in the midst of a storm like that—where the winds are contrary and when we've called on everything we know and it's still not enough—that we learn the second principle: There are going to be times when we just can't "fix" things ourselves!

Following right on the heels of the second principle is the third one: When we realize our own inability to get ourselves out of the storm, we come face to face with the fact that we are *totally* dependent upon Jesus Christ!

Jesus wasn't exaggerating when He said, "Without Me you can do nothing."[3] And yet, until we find ourselves in a storm without any way out, we don't really believe it. Why else would we hang on to certain areas of our lives? It's because deep down we think we can still handle those things ourselves. In the midst of the storm, we learn otherwise. Against the black backdrop of a storm, the light of God's Word shines brighter than at any other time in our lives. And it is then we truly realize that He will never leave us, that He will not abandon us, that we can trust Him with absolutely every area of our lives.

In my own experience, I was wrenched, pulled, and beat down until I got to the point of total dependency upon God. Why did I depend upon God? Because, like the disciples, I had no place else to go. I couldn't get any more treatment because the insurance company would no longer cover me. My income had stopped. And even if I could have paid the doctors, they had already made it clear that there was nothing they could do for me anyway. Everywhere I turned, I seemed to get knocked down again. The winds don't get much more contrary than that, folks!

My storm went on for three long years. It might have seemed to be a similarly long time to the disciples. Remember, they didn't just experience this storm for a few moments—they were out there all night! Jesus didn't come to them until "the fourth watch of the night [sometime between four and six o'clock in the morning]."[4]

## RECOGNIZING "I AM"

Because it was dark, and because Jesus had stayed on the other side, the disciples thought they had to face the storm alone. And for a while, they did. Jesus didn't come to them in the first watch, He didn't come in the second, and He didn't come in the third. The disciples must have felt absolutely abandoned.

They weren't, however, not for a second. In another account of the story, Mark says that while Jesus was praying, He saw the disciples out on the lake.[5] Even in the midst of the worst storms of our lives, when it seems Jesus will never come and rescue us, we are never out of His sight.

But what about when He finally does come to rescue us? We recognize Him immediately and welcome Him with open arms, right? Wrong! At least, that's certainly not what the disciples did. "Now in the fourth watch of the night Jesus went to them, walking on the sea. And when the disciples saw Him walking on the sea, they were troubled, saying, 'It is a ghost!' And they cried out for fear."[6]

The disciples didn't recognize Jesus. Even though they had undoubtedly been crying out to God, wondering when He would come to save them, beginning to despair of ever getting out of the storm alive, they didn't recognize the answer to their prayers when He walked up to them.

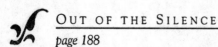

What does that say to us? I believe the principle here is that our prayers aren't always going to be answered quite the way we imagine they will be. And if we don't open ourselves to God's answer coming in His time and in His way, we just might miss that answer altogether!

Now, when Jesus came walking to the disciples on the water, the Bible doesn't actually say how they were able to see Him, but I can imagine lightning illuminating the sky as He approached. Combine that with a loud clap of thunder, and who wouldn't cry out in fear? Sometimes the noise and dangers of the storm can cause so much fear in us that, even when we see Jesus coming toward us, we still don't recognize Him!

Jesus speaks to those fears: "Be of good cheer! It is I; do not be afraid."

None of our modern translations do this verse justice. In the original, what Jesus actually said was, "Don't be afraid; I AM."

I AM is in the midst of the storm. The same I AM who addressed Moses from the burning bush was now walking toward them on the water. Not I WAS or I WILL BE, but I AM. And dear, impetuous Peter calls out, "If you're I AM, tell me to come to you."

It was an incredibly bold statement. If you've ever been surrounded by six- to ten-foot-high swells, you know that the last place you would want to be in that situation is out on the water, but that's what Peter asked, and Jesus called him out on it.

The principle here is that there is going to come a time when our faith needs to be exercised, not just verbalized. The exercising of faith is to do those things that are difficult—even seemingly impossible.

If I exercised any faith in my situation, it was simply that I showed up. When the forum was presented for me to teach, I accepted it. I knew it would be difficult, but I also knew God had called me to teach. So I stepped out onto the platform He provided for me, believing I would stay there as long as He enabled me to do so.

*Duane Miller*

That's what Peter was willing to do. He decided that he'd "show up," even if the stage was a swirling, watery storm.

You know, I've heard people give Peter a hard time for taking His eyes off Jesus and falling into the water and almost drowning. And yet, Peter was the only one who had the courage to get out of the boat at all! And do you know why I think he did that? Because of what Jesus said: I AM is here. Peter realized that, if I AM was standing out on the water, calling him to come, then he most certainly could do just that!

And so he climbed over the edge of the boat, while the other eleven drenched, exhausted, and shivering disciples sat back and said, "Have a nice swim, Peter!" They weren't about to get out of that boat, even though they knew by then that it was going nowhere! This tells me that, every time one person responds to the call of Christ on his or her life, there are at least eleven more who do not. (A sad thought, isn't it?)

## LETTING GO OF THE BOAT

Now the thing to realize about the disciples' boat is that it was no little rowboat. This boat was big enough that, when Peter climbed over the edge, he could still hang on to the side without actually being submerged in the water. And that's an important point, because right there—hanging on to the edge of the boat—is where 90 percent of the church lives about 98 percent of its existence! We've heard Jesus call us; we've figured out that our own talents and abilities just aren't going to get us out of our storm; we know that our only hope is to abandon ship sooner or later, so we crawl over the side—but we just can't get up the courage to let go!

Why? Because to get to Jesus, we're going to have to walk on water—and that's impossible! And yet Jesus is calling us to do it. Are we going to respond, or are we going to spend the rest of our lives hanging on to the side of the boat—a boat that will surely break apart and be destroyed in time?

Peter, however, mustered up the courage to let go. Maybe part of it was that he got sick of listening to the taunts of the

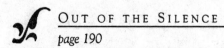

other disciples. But for whatever reason, he let go and began to do the impossible—to walk to Jesus on the water!

But was it really the water he walked on? No. It was the Word of God, spoken by I AM. The Word of God is what held Peter up, and it is what will hold us up in the storms of life. If we don't have God's Word hidden in our hearts, we will never be able to stand on it when troubles come. I'm not sure who said, "Your Word have I hidden in my heart because my heart I have hidden in You," but it is a wonderful truth.

There is a mistaken teaching, which I've heard many times, that says Peter fell when he looked at the waves. When Peter "saw that the *wind* was boisterous, he was afraid; and beginning to sink he cried out, saying, 'Lord, save me!'"[8] (emphasis added). It was not the waves that gave Peter trouble, it was the wind—the same contrary wind that was buffeting the boat!

When the Savior comes to rescue us from the storm, we must let go of the boat and keep our eyes on Him, *even when the circumstances of the storm are still swirling around us!* Often, in the midst of the storm, we will hear Jesus calling to us and begin to respond, only to be stopped when we realize the storm is still raging. The contrary wind didn't cease until Peter had reached Jesus and they both had returned to the boat. Don't miss this principle: When you have prayed for help and the storm seems as if it will never end, don't give up and sink; just keep walking toward Jesus.

Don't let the observation of unchanged circumstances defeat you. I AM has called and is in control. Keep walking!

Notice, too, that when Peter began to sink, all Jesus had to do was reach down to pull him up.[9] Principle? Not only are we always within His sight, but we are always within arm's length of the Lord. Isn't that comforting?

I also appreciate the fact that, even when Peter fell, Jesus didn't leave him in the water to thrash around for a while to teach him a lesson. He reached right down and picked him up. True, Jesus said to Peter, "O you of little faith, why did you doubt?" But I am sure he said it in a loving tone, as a parent to a small, beloved child who has tripped and fallen.

The Bible doesn't tell us how Jesus and Peter got back into the boat; it simply says that, once Jesus rescued Peter from the water, "they got into the boat, [and] the wind ceased."[10] I like to imagine, however, that Jesus and Peter walked back to that boat together, arm in arm—and what a different walk it was from the one Peter had taken alone! Again, don't miss the principle! You see, we cannot walk *with* Jesus until we first walk *to* Jesus. There is no other way. We must let go of the boat and respond to I AM.

## JOY COMES IN THE MORNING

The final principle we need to notice here is what we just read in verse 32: When they got back into the boat, the wind ceased. The storm was over. Peace returned. No storm lasts forever! "For His anger is but for a moment, / His favor is for life / Weeping may endure for a night, / But joy comes in the morning."[11]

The book of Revelation tells us that God will wipe away all our tears.[12] That tells me that, initially, we may arrive in heaven with tears, but God will wipe them away. Now if we tie that together with "Weeping may endure for a night, but joy comes in the morning," that says that, because Jesus is the light[13] and light appears with morning, then there can be no darkness or night or weeping or tears in heaven, because Jesus is there! Where Jesus is, tears are wiped away and rejoicing follows.

The problem comes when we want all the answers now. We want the flesh satisfied in this life, and it just won't happen that way. The most important principle here is, *The storm won't last forever because I AM is in the midst of it!* So whatever the storm may bring—it may even cost me my life—I can still rest in this great truth.

The apostle Paul had an eternal perspective of the kingdom of God. He said: "For to me, to live is Christ, and to die is

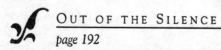

gain."[14] That meant that he did not expect to have every whim of the flesh satisfied on this earth, but he expected to spend an eternity without storms and in celebration with the Anointed One.

Sooner or later, I AM, who is in the midst of the storm with us, is going to bring us through the night and into the morning, where He will wipe away our tears as we rejoice in His presence. And that is the eternal perspective of the kingdom.

I claim no great faith. But I enjoy great grace. The lessons the disciples learned in that storm form a foundation we can all use in dealing with the storms in our lives. In many ways, their story is my story.

# chapter sixteen

# The
# Road Show:
# Showing Up

THE SOUND OF A CAR SQUEAL-ING ITS tires pierces the hot Houston air every weekday afternoon, and it's all my fault.

"Good afternoon, everybody," my voice breaks in. "This is Duane Miller. Welcome to *The Road Show.*"

In one of the ironies of ironies, God has called me into radio. For a man who had virtually no voice for three years, and who was told by the world's best physicians that he would completely lose his voice by 1994 or 1995, isn't it a revelation of God's sense of humor to call me into radio in July of 1996?

Now, tens of thousands of people know me only by my voice!

Five days a week, I sit in my new "office" in the studios of KKHT, "The Word in Texas." The show goes out on 100,000-watt stereo signal to the fourth largest city in America, at prime time for commuters, and has the potential to reach hundreds of thousands of listeners.

God is blessing my current ministry in ways I never could have imagined. During the first week of *The Road Show,* the station manager stopped me and said, "I have great news!"

"What's that?" I asked.

"We've received more response—faxes, phone calls, and letters—from *The Road Show* than we have ever received for a new show."

"Praise the Lord!" I replied.

*The Road Show* might be an apt title for my life since God has healed me. About ten days after my miracle, I met with my Pastor, Dr. John Bisagno, and after rehashing the good news, John said, "We need to find you a church, brother. It's time to get you back in the saddle."

I eagerly agreed, and still would be quite eager to find a pulpit, if only I could end up staying in the same town for at least two weeks in a row. You see, almost immediately after my healing, churches began asking me to come and tell my story. Often, after they hear my testimony, they ask me to come back and teach on something else. So while I still agree with Brother John that going back to a central pulpit seems like a great idea, it's been over three years and I still haven't had the time to update my resume!

I have yet to contact a church on my own and ask to speak, yet in the first 152 days of 1996, I preached 141 times. I've received invitations from virtually every nation, and the only things currently holding me back are that I can only be in one place at one time and I can't always afford to travel overseas.

How long will all this go on? I honestly don't know. As soon as the invitations stop, I'll take that as God's sign that I'm to return to a local pulpit. I don't *need* this ministry, but if God wants to use me this way, I'm determined to be faithful. He's given me a new life, a new voice, and a new story, and I'm prepared to proclaim it wherever there's a hearing.

Our umbrella ministry, "Practical Christianity," has been officially changed to NuVoice Ministries, Inc., although the concept of Practical Christianity will continue to be the theme of what we do. Remember that tiny newsletter I sent out to four hundred people on my Rolodex? It now reaches close to ten thousand homes in fifty states and twenty-two countries.

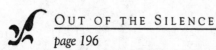

Something else has changed as well. I sit back and watch what has happened, and all of these things absolutely amaze me. You see, God didn't just restore my life, he *amplified* it. He gave me more than my voice back. He gave me access that I never would have enjoyed had I not lost my voice. Think about it—two publishers told me my book would never be published because I couldn't speak, and now, what is it that you're holding in your hands?

I think back to what my father-in-law told me just weeks before I was healed: "Duane," he said, "ultimately, the new ministry God is going to give to you will far outshine your earlier one."

Back then, it was difficult for me to believe him, but he was certainly acting as God's prophet, for all that he has said has come true.

There are difficulties that come along with the increased opportunities, however. Because I went through such a difficult trial, and because I received such a miraculous healing, I'm often given esteem that I haven't really earned. The way I look at it, I just showed up! And if I'd had a choice, I wouldn't have done that!

I don't deserve or want a medal. I didn't choose to lose my voice, and I did nothing to get it back. It wasn't my faith, my virtue, or my purity that led God to heal me. It was solely His sovereign choice, to show the world a picture of how He can remove sin. For that picture to receive its power, I had to go through a difficult and soul-wrenching ordeal. But when God pays back, He pays back in big-time dollars.

NuVoice has witnessed tens of thousands of conversions just in the past three years. This is a confirmation, I believe, of God's word to me that the central message of my healing is about God's forgiveness. Mother Teresa has said that the biggest disease today is not leprosy or tuberculosis but rather the feeling of being unwanted. God has used my disease to cure the social disease of loneliness—for only in a relationship with God can we recover that sense of being wanted.

*Duane Miller*

In fact, evangelism has become such a central part of what we do, that I now regularly tell pastors to expect about 15 percent of the audience to respond to my invitation. If I'm speaking to a crowd of ten thousand people, about fifteen hundred will come forward. If I'm speaking to a small group of fifty, about seven will come forward. It's been so regular, I've just come to expect it.

The wonderful aspect of this response is that a significant portion of it comes from—believe it or not—church members. Many of the people who give their hearts to the Lord have heard literally hundreds of sermons, but still remained, by their own admission, unconverted. I've had diaconate chairmen, choir leaders, and congregational mainstays come forward and tell me they needed to give their hearts to the Lord!

"I don't know the Lord," one deacon told me, "not like what you're talking about, anyway. I don't have that type of relationship, but I want it."

I don't understand why my ministry is so different now, but it is. After speaking at a church in Mississippi, I had deacons in their seventies and eighties come up to me, put their arms around my neck, and with tears in their eyes, say, "This is what church was like when we were boys."

This change in my ministry doesn't come from me or anything I've learned; it comes from the reality of what God has done in my life. I can't write a book called *How to Increase Your Ministry* because the truth is, the only thing that changed was hidden away, cut off from view in the depths of my soul. I wouldn't even know it was there unless I was continually reminded, as I was some months ago when a few Presbyterian pastors approached me after I spoke at one of their meetings. "Duane," they asked, "how do you do it? We don't preach with your power. We have the homiletics down pat, but we just don't have the power."

I didn't know what to tell them. I guess I could tell them, "Okay, here's what you need to do. Get really, really sick so that the virus invades your vocal cords and makes them go limp. Lose your voice for three years. Lose your income. Accumulate amounts of debt you never could have imagined. Watch your entire ministry crash around you. Then, in a sudden burst of God's sovereignty, get healed, and you'll have the power."

For obvious reasons, I don't think my "recipe" would go very far! But I do remember that it was said of Jesus that "He taught them as one having authority, and not as the scribes."[1] Jesus knew who He was, why He was here, and what His message was. In a similar, but certainly far more humble way, He has shown me who I am, why He has allowed me to be here, and what my message is. That security is indeed powerful!

## A VOICE ON THE AIR

Within days of my healing, copies of that tape of my Sunday school class began filling mailboxes across the nation. Friends made copies, our ministry finally began making copies, and soon people I had never met began telling me about how the tape impacted their life.

One of those tapes landed on the desk of Dr. James Dobson of Focus on the Family. It was just a homemade copy, with no voice-over, no professional production, or anything of the kind, but I am told that it moved Dr. Dobson to tears when he listened to it over a weekend. On Monday morning, he tossed the tape on the desk of one of his assistants, and said, "Find this guy. I want him on the show."

The tape didn't have an address, and the person who sent the tape didn't provide one either. The assistant spent several days trying to track me down, but the tape didn't even mention what church I was from.

One afternoon, one of the secretaries overhead Dr. Dobson's assistant saying, "I just can't find this guy!"

"Who?" she asked.

"Duane Miller," he answered. "Dr. Dobson gave me his tape and wants him on the show, but I can't locate him. I've looked everywhere."

"The Duane Miller whose voice was healed?" she asked.

"Yes! You've heard of him?"

"I know his wife."

What are the odds of that?

That's how I got a call in November of 1993. My board went bonkers. "This is great!" they said. "You're going to be on *Focus on the Family!*"

I had begun to see God move in so many wonderful and surprising ways that I guess it just didn't hit me like it hit them. I was eager to meet Dr. Dobson personally, however, and I flew into Colorado Springs in December with great expectations. As I walked into his office, I was surprised at how tall he is—but then, everybody is tall to me.

As we recounted my miracle, Dr. Dobson wept openly. He's a spiritually sensitive man, and it was obvious he had been deeply moved. When people ask me my impressions of Dr. Dobson, I'm always pleased to tell them, "Let me give you some good news. He's exactly what you think he is." He is the same man away from the radio as he is on the radio, and that's about the highest compliment I can give him.

As I walked through the beautiful facilities of Focus on the Family, I was shocked that most everyone had heard my tape. "Your story moved a number of our workers," Dobson told me. "I hope you don't mind if some of our staff sit outside the studio while we tape?"

"Of course not!"

"And would you mind staying afterwards and answering some questions?"

"Absolutely not."

I entered the studio, expecting to see about a dozen people outside the glass-walled studio. Instead, it was packed.

After the program, Dr. Dobson asked me if I ever got angry at God. I didn't even have to think about my response.

"Yes, I got angry," I said, "There were times I wanted to put my fist through the wall. But I never got bitter."

"Why?" Dr. Dobson asked.

"As a boy," I responded, "I had a pastor who taught me, week after week after week, about the sovereignty of God. Now, half the time, I was passing notes to my girlfriend during the sermon, but enough pieces of that truth got through that Duane Miller really does believe in the sovereignty of God. You can't believe in the sovereignty of God and become bitter. You can be angry. You can be frustrated. But if you really believe that God is in control, you can't become bitter."

A few days later, my voice—the voice I thought I would have long since lost—went out to literally millions of Dr. Dobson's listeners *around the world*. Most of these people will never see my face. The only contact they'll have with Duane Miller will be through my voice.

Isn't God amazing?

## THE REST OF THE STORY

Before we close this book, I want to leave you with one more thought. There is no disputing the fact that my ordeal at times felt like walking along the lower regions of hell. It was awful. I would never want to do it again, and I would never wish it on anyone. Even today, I occasionally shudder when I remember those depths of despair.

However, when I think of the tens of thousands of new believers—some who don't even speak English, but who were so moved by the obvious change in my voice on a cassette tape that they became open to a national speaking the gospel in their own language—I have to state unequivocally that all of it was worth it. If just one person became saved as a result of my ordeal, I would gladly do it again. Trading three years of trial for one person's eternal destiny is a pretty good deal by any standard.

I know that many of the people reading this book may be facing a trial that has gone on for much longer than three years. Others of you are in the midst of a more recent trial.

As I look back, all I can share with you is this: God has been blessing my socks off. Virtually every day, I am amazed at the doors He has opened. And I believe God is in His heaven, looking down, and enjoying it all even more than I am.

"How do you like that, Duane?" He must be saying. "And you wanted to come home!"

I've tasted the allure of suicide. It's not an abstraction to me. I've smelled its breath, I've been drawn by its easy release, and through that experience I can say to any of you—those facing physical ailments, relational explosions, financial cataclysm, and vocational rupture—God never stops being God. He has a future for you. Admittedly, for some of you that future may be in heaven, but that's not for you to know, at least not now. Don't short-circuit His process.

Our God is a sovereign God. He's a healing God. He's a faithful God. If my story has taught me anything, it has taught me that.

I've shared with you the reality and genuineness of my experience because I want you to know that God is still on the throne. While that experience was a marvelous one for me personally, I would remind you that God never does anything without purpose. And I believe that His purpose is to encourage you in your faith and to encourage you that God cares about you. He hasn't lost your address.

The story of Duane Miller is the story of a broken man, without hope, who fell headlong into the grace and mercy of a sovereign God. If you don't know that God, please write to us at NuVoice Ministries; we'd be delighted to send you some information. Getting to know God is where healing starts—the kind of healing that counts, anyway.

For those of you who do know the God I'm talking about, may I give you one last word? Trust Him. I know it's hard sometimes. I know it's confusing. I know life can be scary. But remember, the Duane Miller story can be your story—the story of how God not only heals but amplifies. God not only restores, He re-creates.

If He did it for me, He can, and will, do it for you.

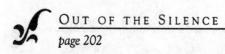

# Notes

Chapter 6
1. Luke 16:10.
2. 2 Kings 14:25.
3. Job 13:15.
4. Se Matt. 11:3.
5. Psalm 77:7-9.
6. John 14:6.

Chapter 10
1. Verses 3-5.
2. 2 Peter 3:9.

Chapter 11
1. Romans 11:33.

Chapter 12
1. Mark 2:8-11.
2. Mark 2:12.
3. Habakkuk 2:2.

Chapter 13
1. Luke 12:48.
2. See Matthew 6:11-12; 7:7-8;
21:22; James 5:16.

Chapter 14
1. Proverbs 25:16; Titus 2:1-2.
2. Hebrews 11:6.
3. See Romans 12:3.
4. Proverbs 13:12.
5. See James 5:13-16.

Chapter 15
1. Matthew 14:22.
2. Matthew 14:24.
3. John 15:5.
4. Matthew 14:25.
5. See Mark 6:48.
6. Matthew 14:25, 26.
7. Matthew 14:27.
8. Matthew 14:30.
9. See Matthew 14:30, 31.
10. Matthew 14:32.
11. Psalm 30:5.
12. See 7:17; 21:4.
13. See Revelation 21:23.
14. Philippians 1:21.

Chapter 16
1. Matthew 7:29.

# About the Author

Duane Miller is the executive director of NuVoice Ministries, Inc. In addition to sharing this testimony with congregations of every denomination, Miller is involved with church-growth consulting and ministers in conferences and crusades across America and around the world. He hosts a daily, one-hour live radio program on KKHT-FM in Houston, Texas. NuVoice Ministries continues to publish the newsletter *Practical Christianity*. He has served as senior pastor of three congregations and has been involved in ministry for more than thirty years.

If you are interested in reaching him or scheduling his ministry in your area, please contact NuVoice Ministries at P.O. Box 27007, Houston, Texas, 77227-7007 or phone 1-800-344-0646.